Infants & Toddlers at Play

Choosing the Right Stuff for Learning & Development

Mary Benson McMullen & Dylan Brody

National Association for the Education of Young Children
Washington, DC

National Association for the
Education of Young Children

1401 H Street NW, Suite 600
Washington, DC 20005
202-232-8777 • 800-424-2460
NAEYC.org

NAEYC Books

**Senior Director, Publishing
& Content Development**
Susan Friedman

Director, Books
Dana Battaglia

Senior Editor
Holly Bohart

Editor II
Rossella Procopio

Senior Creative Design Specialist
Charity Coleman

Senior Creative Design Specialist
Gillian Frank

**Publishing Business
Operations Manager**
Francine Markowitz

Through its publications program, the
National Association for the Education
of Young Children (NAEYC) provides
a forum for discussion of major issues
and ideas in the early childhood field,
with the hope of provoking thought and
promoting professional growth. The views
expressed or implied in this book are not
necessarily those of the Association.

Permissions

NAEYC accepts requests for limited use of our
copyrighted material. For permission to reprint,
adapt, translate, or otherwise reuse and repurpose
content from this publication, review our guidelines at
NAEYC.org/resources/permissions.

Photo Credits

Copyright © Getty Images: cover, iv, 4, 11, 12, 14, 17, 18,
20, 22, 26, 30, 33, 35, 37, 40, 42, 44, 47, 50, 52, 56, 59,
61, 63, 64, 66, 70, 72, 75, 79, 83, 86, 89, 93, 94, 99, 100,
102, 107, 109, 111, and 114

Library of Congress Control Number: 2021933323

ISBN: 978-1-938113-74-1

Item: 1149

Contents

Introduction

Children, after all, are not just adults-in-the-making.
They are people whose current needs and rights
and experiences must be taken seriously.

—Alfie Kohn, *Beyond Discipline: From Compliance to Community*

An Invitation

This book honors and supports the work you—current and future teachers—do, supporting the learning, development, and well-being of children from birth to age 3. With you, we celebrate a passion for the amazing capabilities of children in their first three years of life.

The purpose of this book is to describe and discuss *play materials* (that is, toys and other resources) as the "right stuff" for promoting and supporting learning, development, and a positive sense of well-being through play with very young children. This book is an invitation to think more intentionally about the play materials you select and use for your indoor and outdoor environments and to reflect more deeply on how meaningful and appropriate they are for the individuals in your setting as well as for the group as a whole (NAEYC 2020). Use the ideas in this book to stimulate your own thinking about new ways to see and use familiar, time-honored toys (e.g., balls and dolls) along with newer play materials (e.g., yoga cards and Magna-Tiles).

Reflecting on your role as teacher is also important. You may find it natural and easy to engage fully in play, playful interactions, and meaningful conversations with very young children; for others, this might be more of a struggle. This is especially true if you work with children who are not yet talking—at least not conventionally. In particular, you may find it uncomfortable to speak with a child who may not seem to be talking with you. For some, it may be because you are generally reserved; others may not yet fully understand the importance of these interactions and may worry about looking silly. For those teachers, the play materials and information in this book are meant to offer ways to help you break through the awkwardness or discomfort you may have working with very young children, feel more comfortable holding conversations with them, rediscover what fun it is to play, and feel safe being playful and (yes, sometimes) silly!

We also hope that the play materials in this book and how we present them inspire ways for infant and toddler teachers to communicate clearly to colleagues, families, and administrators about the importance of play and playful interactions and why you want or need certain play materials in your settings. We discuss how to use the materials to create environments and provide experiences that enable each and every child in your group to thrive, flourish, and achieve their full potential. In addition, we ask you to reflect on and consider very carefully the messages communicated by the materials themselves (NAEYC 2019a). Specifically, do the toys and resources demonstrate respect and awareness of the families, languages, cultures, experiences, and abilities and disabilities that are part of your community?

The content in this book reveals our underlying beliefs about the care and education of very young children—namely, infants and toddlers. In this book, our goals are to

> Honor the work and play of children under the age of 3, representing it with respect in what we write, the words of others we share, and the images we show

> Promote play and playful interactions as the major vehicles for scaffolding learning, supporting development, and fostering an overall healthy sense of well-being in very young children (NAEYC 2019b)

> Support the United Nations' recognition of play as a right for all children, including those under the age of 3 (United Nations 1989)

> Acknowledge that children grow, learn, and develop at their own pace and experience their world in their own unique ways (NAEYC 2020)

> Emphasize how although learning and developmental guidelines are useful to frame a broad understanding of what can be expected during the first 36 months of a child's life, they should not be used to define any one individual child because children develop and learn "within specific social, cultural, linguistic, and historical contexts" (NAEYC 2020, 6)

> Reflect a holistic (whole child) approach, recognizing the interconnectedness of growth, development, learning, and well-being across multiple domains (e.g., cognitive, social and emotional, physical)

> Demonstrate respect for the beliefs, backgrounds, languages, and values of children within their families, communities, and cultures (NAEYC 2019a)

> Invest in forming and nurturing strong, positive working relationships with families

> Celebrate the role of those who care for and educate very young children by representing what they do as important and meaningful

> Support a view that focuses on each child in the here and now (their *being*) as equally important—and sometimes even more important—than who they will be in the future (their *becoming*)

About this Book

This book is divided into four main parts. **Part One: Essential Questions** presents foundational information organized around the who, why, how, and what of using play materials to support very young children's learning and development. Chapter 1 describes the changing child over the first three years, focusing on the strengths, needs, and motivations that influence their learning and development. We then talk about the reason play and play materials are important from a child's rights perspective in Chapter 2. Next, we consider the important role you, the teacher, play in supporting learning and development in Chapter 3. The final chapter of Part One, Chapter 4, describes how we organize and present the play materials featured in Parts Two through Four of this book.

The remainder of the book's core content is organized into the following three parts:

> **Part Two: Cognitive Learning and Development**
> **Part Three: Social and Emotional Learning and Development**
> **Part Four: Physical Learning and Development**

Each part includes three chapters that describe suggested play materials and why they are useful for different aspects related to each domain.

All four parts conclude with a brief essay written by infant and toddler professionals (teachers and administrators of programs who serve children from birth to age 3), **In Your Words**.

In **Final Thoughts**, we summarize the key messages in the book and encourage you to consider the information and think about how you would expand on our ideas with further reflection.

We end the book with two appendices to support infant and toddler professionals in their everyday work. **Appendix A** features tables that highlight references and reminders for all teachers about the amazing capabilities of very young children and how they grow and learn over time. **Appendix B** provides a list of recommended children's books for the development and learning domains presented in Parts Two through Four. It is critical to build a collection of children's books that specifically targets the development, learning, and well-being of the children in your group and at the same time reflects their interests, abilities, languages, cultures, and families. This section includes classics, like *The Snowy Day* (by Ezra Jack Keats) and *The Very Hungry Caterpillar* (by Eric Carle), as well as more recent popular books, such as *Press Here* (by Hervé Tullet) and *Sweetest Kulu* (by Celina Kalluk, illustrated by Alexandria Neonakis). We also suggest books that feature diverse children and families, such as *Hands Can* (by Cheryl Willis Hudson, photographs by John-Francis Bourke) and *Mommy, Momma, and Me* (by Lesléa Newman, illustrated by Carol Thompson), and support disabilities, such as *I Can, Can You?* (by Marjorie Pitzer) and *Special People, Special Ways* (by Arlene Maguire, illustrated by Sheila Bailey).

Throughout the book, we define how we use different terms and ideas. We do this to help make this material useful to all teachers, knowing each educator represents a different professional background and works in a different early childhood setting. By taking the space to share definitions and research-based notions of best practices, we hope to empower and inspire you in the work you do.

PART ONE

Essential Questions

CHAPTER 1

Who?

Children from Birth to Age 3

Childhood is not a race to see how quickly a child can read, write, and count. It is a small window of time to learn and develop at a pace that is right for each individual child. Earlier is not better.

—Magda Gerber, *Your Self-Confident Baby: How to Encourage Your Child's Natural Abilities—From the Very Start*

"The overall rate of development in all domains from birth to age 3 is greater than at any other time in life" (McMullen 2013, 32). Just think about it! In less than three years of living on this earth, very young infants—who depend on others to move them from place to place and whose main methods of communicating are robust cries, endearing smiles, and gazing into the eyes of others—become children capable of, among many other things, planning activities, having favorite friends, running, jumping, twirling, climbing, and speaking in full paragraphs. Understanding the rapid nature of the changes over this relatively short period of time helps us appreciate, at any given time or age, what individual children have achieved in terms of learning and development, where they are in the here and now, and what is likely to come in the not-so-distant future. This is vital information for you to have when you plan the next steps for the children in your setting and select which play materials to have available for individual children or the group as a whole (Brazelton & Sparrow 2006; NAEYC 2020).

Because such significant and rapid change occurs during these very early years, in this book we divide the first 36 months of a child's life into four different periods. This is similar to what Bronson (1995) did in the book, *The Right Stuff for Children Birth to 8: Selecting Play Materials to Support Development*. The way we talk about children under age 3 also expands on what Mangione, Lally, and Signer (1990) refer to as the *ages of infancy*, and, like them, we focus on changes in the primary needs and motivations of children. We use the following categories to help us think and talk about very young children:

> **Young infants** (birth to about 6 months)—security seekers

> **Mobile infants** (about 6–8 months to 12–15 months)—discovery seekers

> **Toddlers** (about 10–14 months to 24 months)—autonomy seekers

> **Twos** (about 18–24 months to 36 months)—identity seekers

Primary Needs and Motivations of Children from Birth to Age 3

- **Sense of Security (I am one with the environment):** the sense that the world and those around me are trustworthy and will respond to my needs; priority for young infants

- **Sense of Discovery (I am in an environment with other people and things):** the sense of wonder and excitement from exploration and experience; "aha!" moments of putting language, ideas, and sensory experiences together; priority for mobile infants

- **Sense of Autonomy (I am a person):** the sense of being capable of exploring, discovering, and doing things on one's own and the desire and insistence to make choices; priority for toddlers

- **Sense of Identity (I am this person):** the sense that this is who I am and there are things (including who the people in my family are) that make me different from my friends; priority for twos

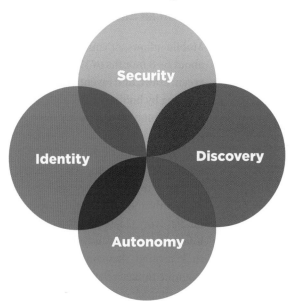

To distinguish young infants, mobile infants, toddlers, and twos, consider how children's needs, motivations, interests, and abilities change over time as they acquire new physical skills, ways of thinking about the world, and an increased ability to socialize and manage emotions. Specifically, young infants are primarily motivated by their search for a sense of security, mobile infants by discovery, toddlers by autonomy, and twos by identity.

Young Infants (Birth to About 6 Months)

I Am One with the Environment

Young, nonmobile infants, from birth to about 6 months or so, are highly dependent on the adults in their lives for where they go and what they experience. While these children are motivated by abilities and needs related to discovery, autonomy, and identity, they are primarily focused on security (Brazelton & Sparrow 2006; Lally 2008). You support young infants' sense of security when they form trusting relationships with you and other key adults who meet their needs promptly, reliably, and in a nurturing manner that is respectful of individual needs and preferences (McMullen 2018). To be secure, young infants need to believe that the environment, their world, is a trustworthy place that responds in a predictable fashion (e.g., when I am hungry, I am fed; when I am upset, I am calmed). Because security needs are most often addressed during routine caregiving during the day (e.g., feeding, diaper changing, preparing for and waking up from naps), these times are opportunities to support young infants' sense of security as you engage with them (Erikson [1950] 2013; Gerber 2003). Trust and security also result from your sensitive responses to their early communications (e.g., crying, facial expressions, body language).

Mobile Infants (About 6-8 Months to 12-15 Months)

I Am in an Environment with Other People and Things

Mobile infants, or children between the ages of about 6–8 months to 12–15 months, usually roll, creep, crawl, and (eventually) begin standing and cruising by holding on to walls and furniture. It is this mobility that helps them construct an understanding that they are separate from other people and things existing alongside them in their environment. Although they are still motivated by a need to seek security and, to a certain extent, autonomy and identity, they are primarily focused on discovery (Lieberman 2017). Because the mobile infant is no longer fully dependent on adults to carry them around, they can now move toward, touch, and examine things, relatively at will. They engage in *sensorimotor discovery*, meaning that they see, hear, touch, taste, and smell everything they encounter.

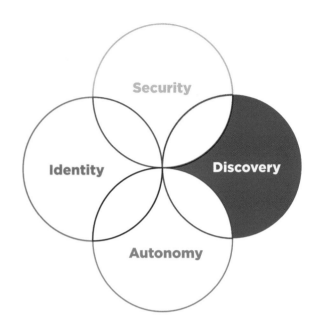

Toddlers (About 10-14 Months to 24 Months)

I Am a Person

The shift into the toddler phase occurs sometime during the second year of life, on average around 12 months of age. A developing mobile infant might become a toddler sometime after they take their first few wobbly steps and walking (or running!) becomes their preferred method of getting around. While security and discovery are still important and motivations and needs based on identity are emerging, toddlers focus most of their energy on autonomy (Brownell & Kopp 2007). Autonomy is all about having control over their own bodies and the choices they make. Toddlers will confidently and quite forcefully declare their independence as persons capable of doing things by themselves; "Me do it!," "No!," and similar pronouncements are probably quite familiar to readers with toddler experience. Practicing independent choice-making allows the toddler to build confidence in their abilities. Model respectful language with a calm tone, and talk to toddlers face-to-face at their level. Any communication concerning their personal needs should be conversational in nature.

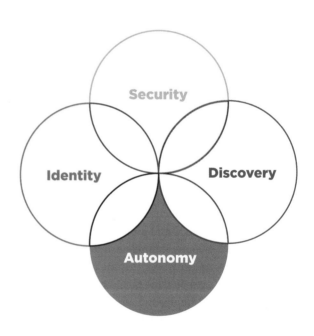

Twos (About 18–24 Months to 36 Months)

I Am this Person

Sometime after 18 months or around their second birthday, toddlers make another developmental shift. This is true, in part, because of obvious physical differences—the 2-year-old is a bigger, stronger version of who they were as a toddler. They often walk with confidence and can also run, jump, dance, and twirl in space. The shift from toddler to 2-year-old is also noticeable because twos become increasingly aware of their identity (who they are), particularly in relation to others, noticing differences and similarities in people. Further, they develop strong preferences for certain friends, wearing particular clothes, doing certain activities, and notably, claiming possession of certain favorite play materials (Zero to Three 2010a). Thus, while twos still need security, love to discover, and crave autonomy, they are most strongly focused on identity.

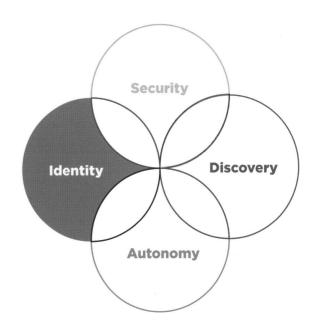

Considering Milestones

Although this book talks about what is typically seen from birth to age 3, children are individuals with their own timetables for acquiring knowledge and skills and reaching developmental milestones. This being said, understanding child development is important in helping you, your colleagues, families, and healthcare professionals think about what might come next and how best to support it (NAEYC 2019b), and it is important for spotting potential problems that may need intervention. Be careful about focusing too much on milestones, resulting in what Batcha (2005) calls "milestone madness." It is primarily for convenience that we refer to average age ranges for common milestones, characterizing changes in behaviors and responses that you may see in the order they are most likely to occur.

CHAPTER 2

Why?

Supporting Learning, Development, and Well-Being

All children are born wired for
feelings and ready to learn.

—National Research Council and Institute of Medicine, *From Neurons
to Neighborhoods: The Science of Early Childhood Development*

The First Years Matter

The way the brain grows and develops during the first three years—whether it is thriving, or not—impacts each and every system in the body for a lifetime. According to the American Academy of Pediatrics, it is the first 1,000 days of life that matter most (Schwarzenberg & Georgieff 2018). During that time, the brain reaches 80 percent of its adult size and becomes the "complex organ that allows children to learn to walk, talk, and read" (Schwarzenberg & Georgieff 2018).

> The first 1,000 days of life—from conception to age three—open a critical and singular window of opportunity. During this period, children's brains can form 1,000 neural connections every second—a once in a lifetime pace never matched again—and these connections are the building blocks of every child's future. (Lake 2017)

Resources About Brain Development

- **Centers for Disease Control and Prevention (CDC):** www.cdc.gov/ncbddd/childdevelopment/early-brain-development.html
- **HealthyChildren.org (from AAP):** www.healthychildren.org
- **Mind in the Making:** www.mindinthemaking.org
- **Start Early:** www.startearly.org
- **Zero to Three:** www.zerotothree.org/espanol/brain-development

Beginning in the 1990s, rapid advancements in neurobiological research, largely from new technologies that allowed us to "see" into the brain, created an explosion of interest. This keen interest resulted in two highly influential works: *Rethinking the Brain: New Insights into Early Development* (Shore 2003) and *From Neurons to Neighborhoods: The Science of Early Childhood Development* (NRC & IOM 2000). These works scientifically confirmed many things that early childhood professionals had already learned through experience about what really matters in supporting children's healthy growth, development, and learning, including the following:

> The first five years of life are important in laying the foundation for all later learning, and the first three years of life are especially important.

> Neural pathways and networks grow through repeated experiences, and the strength of the connections and what is remembered and learned can be impacted by strongly positive (or negative) emotions.

> Quality environments that stimulate the brain and close, positive, caring relationships between adults and children nourish the brains of very young children and optimize their overall growth, development, learning, and well-being.

> Playing, singing, holding conversations, and reading with very young children are every bit as important as healthy food and a safe, clean environment.

Who the Child Is Now and Who They Will Become Both Matter

The "Convention on the Rights of the Child" (United Nations 1989) and child's rights advocates (e.g., Uprichard 2008) urge us to focus on young children as human *beings* (who they are in the here and now), as well as human *becomings* (who they may be in the future). In this book, *being* is defined primarily in terms of supporting the well-being of very young children as "a general state of being and feeling well overall, in terms of physical and psychological health and safety, emotional stability and soundness, and overall satisfaction with activities and relationships within the group" (McMullen, Buzzelli, & Yun 2016, 262). Thinking about who the child is becoming helps you focus on preparing them for whatever the future may bring, whether that future is near or far. *Becoming* implies change, or the movement toward something new and different.

Taking a child's rights perspective means recognizing that very young children have the right to

> Mindful practices and equitable learning spaces

> Be and become without shame or prejudice

> Make mistakes, feel their feelings, and have bad days

> Have a clear sense of well-being

> Witness and engage in healthy relationships

> Be respected as unique individuals and complete persons who identify and feel proud of who they are (NAEYC 2019a)

Changes Over Time

The rapid and significant changes that occur throughout the first three years of life are a result of three distinct but highly interrelated processes: growth and maturation, development, and learning.

Defining Terms That Relate to Changes During the First Three Years

- **Growth** involves physical changes in the body in ways that are mostly observable and measurable in terms of amounts, such as size and weight, length or height, number of teeth, and head circumference.

- **Maturation** refers to the timing and rates of change related to growth of physical (i.e., body and brain), cognitive, and emotional structures and functions; for instance, the timing of when a young infant's eyes focus clearly beyond 12 inches or a toddler achieves bladder control.

- **Development** is driven by growth and maturation that occur during interactions and experiences in the world, which range from simple to increasingly complex and include facing physical challenges, communicating, thinking and problem solving, and feeling about and relating to oneself and others.

- **Learning** is dependent on the growth, maturation, and development of the brain and is often defined as a relatively lasting change in behavior, knowledge, or skill that results from experience, teaching, or practice.

Growth and Maturation

The term *growth* refers to all physical changes that occur over time in the body that are observable and measurable, including size and weight, length or height, number of teeth, and head circumference (Gerber, Wilks, & Erdie-Lalena 2010). The term *maturation* refers to the timing and rates of change to body structures and functions that occur alongside growth and are determined by internal biological factors. Whereas growth refers only to physical systems, maturation involves cognitive and emotional systems as well (Berk & Meyers 2015). How a child grows and matures, and at what rate, is determined genetically long before birth, and it will play out as directed by their DNA unless the child experiences malnutrition or exposure to harmful chemicals, drugs, or other toxins (Center on the Developing Child, n.d.). Examples of changes due to growth and maturation include the following:

> Young infants' first teeth erupt in their gums between 4–7 months.

> The excretory system matures between 24–30 months, allowing young children to achieve full and voluntary bladder and bowel control.

No amount of adult intervention or involvement will make the very young child grow or mature more quickly.

Development

Development refers to changes the child undergoes that move them from simple to increasingly complex ways of adapting to the world (Berk & Meyers 2015). During the first three years, children develop new ways of thinking and problem solving, increasingly more efficient means of moving about in the environment, and more complex techniques for handling their emotions and relating to others. The mind and body work together as very young children experience the environment and everything in it. The brain starts organizing information from all of the senses—sight, smell, touch, taste, and hearing—to make sense of what things are and how things work. Examples of changes due to development include the following:

> Between about 4–7 months of age, young and mobile infants develop a sense of *object permanence*; that is, the understanding that even if they cannot see a person or object, they continue to exist.

> At around age 2½, children move from solving all of their problems in a *sensorimotor fashion* (or physically manipulating objects and thinking as they do) to being capable of *symbolic thinking*, which allows them to hold mental images in their head and think about things before acting.

Although you may be able to hurry along the achievement of some developmental milestones, why rush? Although training a child to crawl, walk, or say *mama* might result in that child beating their own internal clock by a few days or a couple of weeks, why does it matter? Is it for the child's benefit? Did they enjoy the process? Rather, we urge you to provide environments, experiences, and play materials that support development as it unfolds.

Infants and Toddlers at Play

Learning

Learning refers to relatively stable changes that occur in behaviors, knowledge, and skills. Unlike growth and maturation, which are most strongly—but not exclusively—determined by genetics (nature), learning, like development, is primarily influenced by experiences and relationships within the environment (nurture) (McMullen 2013). It is now widely accepted that nature and nurture work together to advance children's abilities and understandings of the world around them. What does matter is that you understand that learning occurs constantly as children interact within their environments through play and engage with other people and things. Examples of changes due to learning include the following:

> By receiving predictable, reliable, and sensitive responses, young infants learn that the world around them is trustworthy and that their needs will be met quickly and respectfully.

> After carefully watching their teachers at lunch, over time, toddlers start to use sign language, having learned the gestures for words such as *more, done,* and *milk.*

CHAPTER 3

How?

The Role of Teachers

Lure babies into activities just a wee bit
difficult, puzzling, different, more complex . . .
stretch their persistence and determination
to try new tasks or more complex toys.

—Alice Sterling Honig, "For Babies to Flourish," paper presented at
the Anniversary Meeting of the American Montessori Society

Teaching very young children can be wonderfully rewarding, and it can also be challenging.
One challenge is being taken seriously as educators. Teachers share that they are often called
upon to explain to others how the work they do with very young children is educational
(Goouch & Powell 2013). People outside the field may see "just" a lot of free play combined
with caretaking, such as feeding, diapering, and napping. Early childhood educators know the
critical importance of these activities and routines and understand that they have everything
to do with teaching and learning. They understand that *everything* we do with very young
children *is* teaching them things—very important things—and providing lessons that last a
lifetime. Teaching and learning happen when you have a deep conversation with a young
infant on the changing table, encourage a newly mobile infant to crawl toward you, blow
bubbles with a group of toddlers, or facilitate a gardening project with 2-year-olds.

There are several ways you facilitate learning and development while supporting the well-being
and well-becoming of children. Educators embrace developmentally appropriate practice
(DAP) by "building on each child's strengths" using teaching approaches and methods that are
"culturally, linguistically, and ability appropriate for each child" (NAEYC 2020, 5). Also, you
"understand that teaching young children requires skills and strategies that are responsive to
and appropriate for individual children's ages, development, and characteristics and the social
and cultural family contexts in which they live" (NAEYC 2019b, 17).

The Importance of Observation

Being responsive requires a consistent practice of ongoing observation to understand what the
child is learning within their play, what teaching strategies might be helpful, and when to use
these strategies and tools. Allowing play to be child directed provides moments for teachers to
observe and reflect on the child's development and learning while staying close and connected.

When you observe children, you gain (NAEYC 2020)

> Information to connect with the child

> Insight about who they are as an individual

> Opportunities to connect past learning experiences to the current moment

> Knowledge for planning a meaningful curriculum that is culturally responsive

Observation is an insightful evaluation tool for determining how a child responds to interactions, play materials, and stimulation within their play. By observing a child as they play, you can see when they may need a new form of guidance beyond a verbal explanation, when they look uncertain (signaling that they need direct scaffolding), or patterns in their play that suggest more hands-on modeling might be needed.

There are many reasons why a young child may throw a block, for example, but close observation will help you determine whether this is rooted in boredom; a desire to explore the properties of physics; a physical need to throw and use their upper body; a signal that the child has an unmet need like feeling hungry, tired, frustrated, or lonely; or a cue that the child may benefit from you moving closer to provide support for a new building project. What you notice during these moments can also show when it might be time to move furniture to provide access to play materials or create spaces throughout the room where the child can work uninterrupted. Observation is a practice of understanding the needs of the child and finding pathways that can connect them to success and well-being.

Best practices require teachers to have a variety of methods they can pull from to meet the individual developmental and learning needs of the children in their care. Although observation is one critical tool in establishing each child's needs and areas of growth, teaching methods that nurture relationships will bring more nuance and depth to a child's learning experience than observation alone can. Next, we explore the varied ways you can support young children through individual exploration, social learning through shared experiences, and direct guidance and instruction.

Individual Exploration

You facilitate individual exploration by preparing environments to include play materials that address the interests, needs, and motivations of each and every child in the group (Bergen, Reid, & Torelli 2008). Free and uninterrupted exploration time allows children to choose activities and experiences that are personally meaningful and enjoyable to them (Dewey [1938] 1997; NAEYC 2019b). Individual exploration allows children to take time to experiment with and construct knowledge about different things and practice new skills on their own. The play materials you provide encourage children to take the next small steps on their own personal development and learning journeys (Piaget & Inhelder 1969; Tryphon & Vonèche 2016). You also play a role in making sure that the play materials available to children offer challenges but do not cause them to become overly frustrated (NAEYC 2020).

Social Learning Through Shared Experiences

Social learning theorists, such as Vygotsky, help us understand the power of learning both from and with others (Bodrova & Leong 2006). Whether it's you with one child, one child with another in a pair, or you with a small or large group, working and playing with and alongside others and sharing experiences together allows children to co-construct knowledge and skills across all learning and development domains. Highlighted next are two important types of social learning you can use when working with children under 3: modeling and scaffolding.

Modeling

Very young children are excellent at observing and imitating other children and adults who serve as models of how to communicate, relate, behave, and problem solve (Bandura 1976; Kolodziej 2015; Loveless, n.d.; Stiefel 2005). *Modeling* is a way for you to support prosocial behaviors, such as sharing and helping others (Brownell et al. 2016). If you stay observant, you will see very young children engage in behaviors that seem far beyond their years, such as returning a dropped pacifier to a younger child, giving a favorite stuffed animal to a distraught peer, or talking into a block held to their ear as if it is a telephone—all behaviors they have learned by watching others do similar things. Because children might imitate any experience, do your best to model behaviors and language that you hope to see in the children in your care. You can capitalize on children's strong ability to observe and their desire to imitate by encouraging ways of being and ways of doing things within your setting.

Scaffolding

The building construction metaphor of *scaffolding* is used to describe how you can "support children's development and learning by offering just the right help at just the right time in just the right way" (Gillespie & Greenberg 2017, 90). Scaffolding is a term that came from those who studied Vygtosky. Another related Vygotskian idea is the *zone of proximal development* (ZPD) (Bodrova & Leong 2006; Jung & Recchia 2013). The most straightforward way to think about ZPD is as the space (or zone) that exists between what children can learn to do or come to understand on their own and what they can learn to do or come to understand with some kind of assistance. That assistance is the scaffolding, or the support, you provide to help the child reach the top of the zone. Although teachers scaffold learning and development, remember that peers and materials do as well (NAEYC 2020).

It is a delicate dance of knowing what will work for a child, at what time, and in which ways that will be most meaningful. Scaffolding extends play, reintroduces familiar concepts within new or different types of situations, expands engagement, and allows children to experience the delight of successfully meeting challenges. This might look like placing certain play materials just out of reach of a young infant, which encourages them to use their core muscles and practice their hand–eye coordination as they reach for what they are interested in. You are scaffolding when you add hand motions to a familiar and beloved song while singing with mobile infants, offer materials for a toddling child to hold as they work on steadying their steps, or say words such as *open* and *twist* when 2-year-olds use containers with lids at the sensory table.

Direct Guidance and Instruction

Another way that you facilitate learning and development is by providing guidance about expectations and behaviors and directly communicating information, concepts, and specific facts (Dean & Gillespie 2015). Direct guidance and instruction may be part of scaffolding or may simply occur as part of your daily routine, such as when you help children learn how to function within group care. At all times, embody a philosophy of respect for children and an intention to help them.

Asking a toddler to "Please roll the ball to me," or saying to a 2-year-old, "Please put the book back on the shelf," are examples of respectful direct guidance or instruction. It also occurs when you

> Ask an older infant to help in their caregiving (e.g., "Please reach your arms up high so I can get your shirt off")

> Remind a mobile infant not to grab the hair of a peer (e.g., "Please be gentle")

> Offer toddlers paper towels to clean the tabletop

> Sit beside 2-year-olds and explain each motion of using scissors in a safe way

> Encourage children under 3 to participate in hygiene routines (e.g., "Hold your hands under the water; that's right, it's time to wash hands so you can stay healthy")

Although many of these examples are verbal guidance and instruction, it is important to supplement verbal cues with other forms of guidance that are developmentally appropriate and meet the individual needs of the child. Give young children physical or visual cues, such as gestures, body language, and facial expressions, to give further context to support the child. For example, the mobile infant may not yet understand what being gentle means in practice. Provide a physical cue along with verbal guidance by gently brushing the child's hand as you discuss how they can care for their friend.

Putting It All Together

In practice, all of these methods of learning and development happen at the same time in busy birth-to-3 settings. Some children may be engaged in individual exploration in a space you and your colleagues carefully prepared that morning, another may be patting a baby doll the way she knows her teachers do before nap, while yet another is being scaffolded by a teacher who offers kind encouragement and just a bit of direct guidance as she tries to unravel the mysteries of the shape sorter.

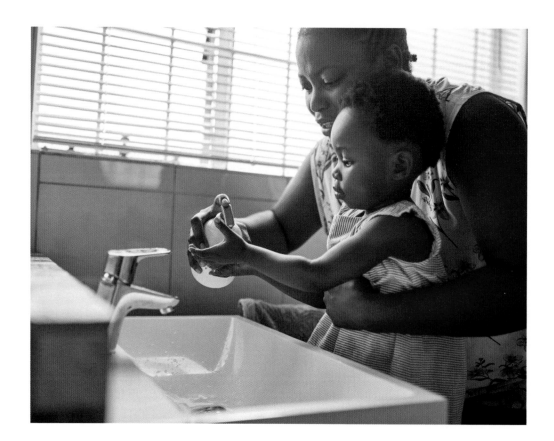

How can you connect to each of these important ways of learning that swirl around children every day? How can you achieve balance between scaffolding and allowing space for the child to develop on their own timeline? The discussions of play materials in future chapters focus on observation as the bridge that connects the following three important roles you have:

> Developing and nurturing individualized, strengths-based relationships with each child and family

> Providing flexible curriculum with mindful use of teaching and learning methods

> Setting up and continuously adapting the learning environment and play materials to allow every child in the group to have optimal development, learning, and positive well-being (NAEYC 2020)

Careful observation gives you the clarity to distinguish between moments when children need your support and when not to intrude in learning moments that are deliciously unfolding for the child as they play contentedly on their own (Forman & Hall 2005; NAEYC 2020). "Educators support and extend children's play experiences by providing materials and resources based on careful observation of children's play choices" (NAEYC 2020, 21).

It is important to always remember that what works for one child may not necessarily work for another. This is the beauty and the challenge of individualized care. It takes time and effort to recognize and craft what is needed from moment to moment. This is done by taking note of individual children's interests, abilities, and cultures, as well as observing what sustains their attention, how they respond to interactions, and what causes them to end their play or become overstimulated (ECLKC 2020).

As a teacher, you provide play materials that are developmentally appropriate and respond to children's feedback to see what changes need to be made (Bergen, Reid, & Torelli 2008; NAEYC 2020). When children show you that a space or play material no longer serves their needs and interests, pay attention to these calls for change. Maybe you notice that materials seem to invite inappropriate or dangerous play, certain times of the day or places in which children become overstimulated or upset, or an area in your setting is congested or includes play materials that seem unused or uninteresting to children.

In essence, how to teach can be summed up by the following: Get to know the children, observe their work and interactions, offer individualized support, create spaces to help each child thrive, constantly assess how play materials and spaces are being used by paying attention to children's feedback, and update and change play materials to keep learning and development alive.

CHAPTER 4

What?

Curating Play Materials for Very Young Children

Play reveals children's interests and nourishes the growing edges of their competence. [...] Specific features of the play materials provided are also important.

—Martha B. Bronson, *The Right Stuff for Children Birth to 8: Selecting Play Material to Support Development*

This book defines *play materials* for very young children as toys and resources that support development, learning, and well-being through play in both indoor and outdoor environments. *Toys* are objects that children use in play, such as balls and dolls, small handheld vehicles, and stuffed animals. *Resources* are objects used in play that are not categorized as toys but do support playful learning and enjoyment, such as art supplies (e.g., crayons, easels, markers, paints, paper) and furniture and equipment (e.g., slides, swings, tables). Resources also include abstract assets like your responsive interactions with a child or a group of children, an anti-bias approach to teaching, purposeful learning spaces, time you provide in the daily schedule for free play and exploration, and the richness of opportunities within the environment.

Defining What Play Materials Are

Play materials for very young children are **toys** and **resources** that support development, learning, and well-being through play in both indoor and outdoor environments.

Toys: Objects that children use in play (e.g., balls, blocks, dolls, rattles, stuffed animals)

Resources: Objects that are used in play but are not categorized as toys, including art supplies (e.g., crayons, easels, markers, paints, paper) and furniture and equipment (e.g., slides, swings, tables), as well as abstract assets that support play (e.g., dedicated time in the daily schedule for free play and exploration, focused attention from teachers, an anti-bias approach to teaching, purposeful learning spaces, richness of opportunities presented in the environment, responsive interactions with you and with other children)

Selecting Toys and Resources for Play

Just as the curator of a museum exhibit selects artistic works and artifacts and determines how best to display them, as curators of play materials, we gave careful thought about what to feature in this book and the best way to describe how and why to use them. We first considered the possibilities, and then purposefully selected examples that support the learning, development, and positive well-being of children under the age of 3. Our selections and how we present them are meant to inspire ideas about similar materials that could be used to accomplish the same goals in a given category, as well as how the materials could be used in different ways with different age groups.

Foremost in our minds was selecting play materials that show respect for very young children and their capabilities. By that we mean that the things we recommend are intended to challenge children's emerging skills and abilities without being so difficult that they cause children stress and frustration. Of course, the materials are also fun and enjoyable, since we know from brain research that children learn best when they experience strong positive emotions (NRC & IOM 2000).

Additionally, we feature play materials that are

> Developmentally appropriate

> Positive reflections of children's home languages, cultures, families, and communities

> Affordable

> Washable

> Strong and durable

> Nontoxic

> Safe, with no rough or sharp edges or small parts that can break off

> Open-ended and multifaceted

> Nonelectronic

> Not too small and not too big

> Limited in the number of pieces and parts they have

> Timeless (i.e., has had or is expected to have enduring popularity)

Choking Hazards

According to the American Academy of Pediatrics (AAP 2010), toys and materials used with children under age 3 should meet US Child Safety Protection Act standards for small parts. This requires that objects be at least 1.25 inches in diameter and between 1 and 2.25 inches in length. Balls and other round objects should be at least 1.75 inches in diameter. The simple and inexpensive small parts test fixture (SPTF) can be used to test the safety of objects. If the object fits completely within the SPTF, it is too small for children under age 3.

Presenting Play Materials

After identifying and selecting play materials to feature, we considered how best to present or cluster them to be as useful and meaningful as possible. Ultimately, we decided to organize them based on their primary role in supporting learning, development, and positive well-being in the following three domains:

> **Cognitive** (*I learn how things work*): involves growth and change in intellectual and mental abilities such as thinking, remembering, reasoning, problem solving, and understanding

> **Social and emotional** (*I learn who I am and how I feel*): refers to understanding self, establishing positive and rewarding relationships with others, and learning to express and regulate emotions and understand them in others

> **Physical** (*I learn how to move and do things*): includes development of perceptual (i.e., taking in and being able to use sensory information) and motor (i.e., balance and control and understanding movement of all parts of the body) skills

Some of the play materials in this book support more than one domain; similarly, many may be appropriate for one or more age groups. In an effort to avoid too much repetition, individual materials are featured in the most relevant categories. We encourage you to be flexible and creative in your thinking about how best to use the materials suggested to support more than one area of learning and development and to be fluid in your consideration of each item's age appropriateness.

Language and communication are a critical part of the cognitive, social and emotional, *and* physical domains—you cannot separate them! In the following chapters on play materials for each of these domains, we emphasize how development, learning, and well-being are supported by and along with language (both verbal and nonverbal) and communication (i.e., the child's ability to understand and use language effectively to get their needs met and hold back-and-forth conversations with others).

Within each of the three main domains covered in Parts Two, Three, and Four, play materials are further organized around selections that are most relevant and appropriate for young infants, mobile infants, toddlers, and twos. Featured materials were selected based on how they address growth and development expectations, as well as the strengths, needs, motivations, and behaviors of children as they grow and mature from birth to age 3. In addition, we gave careful consideration to how the materials reflect children's languages, cultures, families, and communities and accommodate a variety of disabilities. Young children establish a more secure sense of belonging with their teachers and other children in settings that affirm their cultural identities and unique personhood. This affirmation can come in many forms, from selecting bilingual books that reflect the diverse home languages of the children and families in your setting to adapting messy art activities for children with sensory sensitivities. Your space should honor and reflect the daily lives, needs, and cultures of the children and families you serve.

Always remember that age range distinctions are guidelines only. Because development is an individual process, some children may want or need to play with materials that some might see as more appropriate for younger children or begin experimenting with and getting to know materials meant for older children. Child development rarely occurs in a straight line, and how individual children learn and develop often varies from these broad general guidelines. They are primarily useful to help in understanding the general direction of changes that usually occur over the first three years and are not to be used to identify deficits or diagnose a developmental delay or disability. Rather, we simply hope to provide a way of thinking about what children have accomplished to get to the here and now (i.e., their being) as well as an awareness of where they may be going (i.e., their becoming).

In Your Words

Leah Bruton, a teacher at the Explore + Discovery Early Learning Center in New York City, reflects on her role as an educator of infants.

. . . .

Throughout my journey as a teacher, I have come to understand our most important role as teachers is to be facilitators and joyful observers of children's lives and development. I learned to trust the infant as a scientist who has the drive, initiative, and ability to make and test hypotheses about their world. This trust allows them the freedom to explore materials on a deep level and promotes mastery through exploration.

The teachers at our center value long periods of continuous time throughout the day to allow in-depth play with quality materials. We slowly make additions and modifications that are necessary or meaningful and are based on our observations as opposed to predetermined weekly plans. This approach demonstrates a real appreciation for the depth of knowledge the children have and are acquiring. We are especially proud of creating successful opportunities for block play over the past two years. We are continuously surprised by the innovation and skilled building we see in the block area. We believe that the strong relationships between children and staff fueled deeper engagement and learning over time.

In my room, I introduced blocks and other toys in baskets during the summer before children transitioned to the twos' room. A 19-month-old child had set up cylinders in descending order by size on the windowsill. She found a round block that fit perfectly to extend the set. Seeing this child's creativity and understanding was a powerful visual reminder for me to never limit what I think children are noticing or absorbing.

At the beginning of this year, I offered a limited, curated selection of blocks for children to explore. I observed the children transporting, stacking, and lining up the blocks, and creating enclosures. *The Block Book* was my guide to a quality block area. I simplified the ideas to create a space where the children could build collaboratively. At first, I offered fewer shapes and numbers of each block to facilitate building. I gradually added more blocks and until one-third of the room was devoted to building. I found that incorporating toys from other areas in the room is the key to engaging many children in the block area. I saw baby dolls in beds, cars in garages, and eventually the symbolic use of blocks for goats in a pen. I offered drawing materials in the block area as a way to engage children's creativity and interest in writing. I saw the children experience learning across the developmental domains in the block area.

Using the child's interests to create added excitement about blocks was a very successful way to extend engagement. How I handled the children bringing materials into the block area has become an important and recurring topic in our team meetings. I believe the children needed the freedom to incorporate materials from throughout the room and our trust as they experimented. I acknowledged the crucial role of teachers as engaged observers. I wanted to give the children as much freedom as possible while maintaining a safe environment. For instance, in the block area are two big beautiful windowsills. The children love building on these windowsills with the blocks that have colored Plexiglas shapes. Being rough on the window or on the windowsill is a boundary that is frequently tested. I feel it is important to allow the children the freedom to build on the windowsill, while at the same time providing predictable limits within a fluid boundary.

I expected that blocks would provide a rich backdrop for math and spatial reasoning learning to occur. Over time, I was pleased to see evidence of learning across all domains.

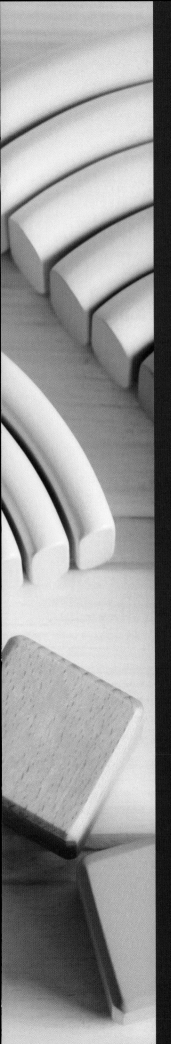

PART TWO

Cognitive Learning and Development

Suggested Play Materials

- Balls (e.g., knobby, squishy, with bells and chimes)
- Bubbles
- Busy boards or boxes and activity cubes
- Finger paints and foams
- Grasping toys to hold, shake, and squeeze
- Images with patterns, different shapes, and contrasting colors
- Mobiles hung from a floor stand (i.e., baby gyms)
- Molded plastic animals (e.g., bugs, dinosaurs, forest critters, sea creatures)
- Music representing different cultures and styles
- Musical instruments (e.g., simple and safe bells, shakers, drums, tambourines)
- Rattles, teethers, and things to chew on and taste
- Rugs, mats, and fabrics with different textures
- Scarves and fabric pieces
- Sensory bottles
- Sensory tables and tubs
- Smell jars, bottles, and cups

CHAPTER 5

Play Materials That Help Me Construct Knowledge and Understanding

Children are born learning.

—Andrew Meltzoff, "Born to Learn: What Infants Learn from Watching Us," *The Role of Early Experience in Infant Development*

Jean Piaget (1896–1980) and Lev Vygotsky (1896–1934) are well known for their theories of cognitive development in young children. Both Piaget and Vygotsky spoke about how learning and development occur as children build (construct) knowledge and understanding of people and things in the world around them (Semmar & Al-Thani 2015). Piaget said children do this using all of their senses as they play with materials on their own, and Vygotsky stressed that it happens best when children directly interact with others while exploring their environment.

The Other Senses

Along with the commonly known five senses (sight, sound, touch, smell, and taste), there are two that are less well known:

- The **vestibular sense** involves movement and balance and gives the child information about where their body is in space.

- The **proprioceptive sense** tells the child where their various body parts are in relation to each other and other things at any given time.

The play material suggestions in this chapter support cognitive learning and development that happen when children use one or more of their senses to construct knowledge and understanding. This happens best when children are free to move their bodies in the ways they want, which results in the movement and sensory parts of the brain working together in what is called *sensorimotor learning* (von Hofsten & Rosander 2018). Sensorimotor learning supports three important areas of cognitive development in infants and toddlers—sensory integration, object permanence, and focused attention—which are also supported by the play materials featured in this chapter.

Key Sensorimotor Developments

- **Sensory integration:** When two or more senses are used at the same time, the brain integrates, or combines, the information to understand what has happened and then guides responses.
- **Object permanence:** The understanding that objects and people continue to exist even if they cannot be seen or heard.
- **Focused attention:** The amount of time a child can ignore distractions and focus on a person, object, or event is driven by how interesting something is (Ruff & Capozzoli 2003). Focused attention increases about three to five minutes each year.

Young Infants (Security Seekers)

Sensory stimulation is a need as important as food and oxygen to a young infant! However, too much of anything, even a good thing, can have negative consequences. Because a young infant's neurological system is still maturing, they can easily become overstimulated, particularly in a busy, noisy (and often smelly!) child care setting. "Overstimulation happens when a child is swamped by more experiences, sensations, noise, and activity than she can cope with" (Raising Children Network 2020). As you consider play materials for young infants, keep in mind the need for balance between too little sensory stimulation, which may result in a bored and disengaged young infant, and too much, which may cause needless stress.

Attention-Grabbing Toys

Young infants' visual ability grows rapidly over the first few weeks. Between 3 and 4 months, young infants begin to track (visually follow) objects or people that move across their field of vision, even from across the room, until they disappear (Berk & Meyers 2015). At this age, out of sight means out of mind in terms of the development of object permanence. You can observe changes in visual ability, object permanence, and gradual increases in attention span by shaking a rattle in the child's line of sight. The sight and the sound together will attract their attention. Slowly and smoothly move the rattle while shaking it, first in one direction, back to the middle starting point, and then in the other direction. Other items that attract young infants' attention and stimulate them include blocks, books, and cards that show images of faces, simple patterns and shapes, or contrasting colors.

As their teacher, your role is to engage young infants in joint attention experiences (Degotardi 2017). *Joint attention* "enables infants to communicate with adults as well as with each other, sharing what is in their minds" as they attend to some third thing together (Shin 2012, 309). When you hold young infants in your arms or lap, they are highly motivated to look at things. Encourage them with your words, using soft and soothing tones, while pointing to interesting

things. Similarly, you can join a young infant who is already intently gazing at something on their own and begin a joint attention experience by recognizing what they are already looking at, turning your own eyes toward it and commenting on it.

Things to Touch, Taste, and Smell

Families often ask, sometimes with frustration, "Why does my baby put everything in their mouth?!" As you know, mouthing is one of the primary ways that very young children come to understand the properties of objects. As they examine objects with their mouths, infants feel the textures and contours and experience the various tastes and smells of the objects. To support this learning, have plenty of safe toys that can be grabbed, held in one hand, mouthed, and retrieved after children lose interest in them so the toys can be sanitized. Rugs and mats with different textures (e.g., soft, scratchy, sticky, shaggy) are also wonderful for young infants. The fabrics and materials stimulate touch receptors in their skin as infants encounter them with fingers, hands, feet, and any other unclothed parts of their bodies. Place young infants on their tummies on surfaces with eye-catching features, such as water mats with floating toy fish or blankets with clear pocket panels that can hold photos of families or animals. Such materials stimulate touch and visual senses as well as hearing when you engage with infants in the experience.

Mobile Infants (Discovery Seekers)

Mobile infants are all about discovery. It is a period of wonder and excitement as mobile infants move about experiencing one "aha!" moment after another as they put language, ideas, and sensory experiences together. This discovery learning is aided both by their increased mobility and continuing maturation of vision and depth perception that allows them to see things in three dimensions.

Sensory Bottles and Bubbles

Play materials that are particularly interesting to mobile infants and promote sensory integration and focused attention are sensory bottles and bubbles. A sensory bottle is a see-through container (e.g., an unbreakable jar, a sealed bottle, a plastic tube) that holds an interesting object that floats and moves through it. There are many different toys like this on the market, of course, but you can make them using directions suggested on numerous websites. This is also true of bubble solutions.

When mobile infants play with sensory bottles or bubbles, it is usually one-on-one or in a small group with you. These materials provide wonderful opportunities to experience a few quiet and peaceful moments of joint attention and conversation as the children watch what happens when you blow bubbles into the air or gently tip the bottle over or from side to side. These play materials typically mesmerize mobile infants, and the interesting nature of such activities may help them build on their developing ability to filter out distractions and focus or pay attention longer. Following bubbles or the objects in a sensory bottle as they float about supports the mobile infant's visual tracking skills. As mobile infants try to catch the floating bubbles, the movement of their hands connects the hand–body movement (proprioception) to the visual sense. When the mobile infant finally catches a bubble, they feel a wetness and stickiness and smell the soapy scent of the bubble water, aiding in their construction of understanding of what bubbles are all about.

Balls That Are Knobby, Squishy, or Have Bells and Chimes

Balls of different sizes and materials are great for mobile infants. They can facilitate and support all areas discussed in this chapter related to cognitive learning and development: sensory stimulation and integration, object permanence, and focused attention. Balls are responsive, and mobile infants quickly learn that balls—or at least most of them—roll in a predictable way. As the mobile infant follows a ball's movement across the floor or grass, they can practice their rapidly maturing visual tracking skills. When the movement of a ball is paired with the sound of a chime or a bell from inside the ball, the mobile infant's brain has to integrate the two senses that are stimulated—sight and hearing—strengthening the sensory integration of the experience. If the ball disappears partially from view, the mobile infant's developing understanding of object permanence allows them to go after it and retrieve it. In terms of the development of object permanence, the child still needs to see at least some of the object to know that it still exists.

Peekaboo, I See You!

Peekaboo is a simple game to play with both young and mobile infants. Not only is it fun, it also works to strengthen visual tracking, supports the development of object permanence, and can help mobile infants work through issues of separation anxiety. They come to understand that even if a favorite person disappears, they can reappear too!

Toddlers (Autonomy Seekers)

When toddlers start to walk at around 10–14 months, they begin a new way of seeing and experiencing the world. Along with it comes a growing, and sometimes urgent, need for autonomy. Toddlers like the sense of power and strength that comes from doing things on their own and making their own choices. Up to this point, they have been developing knowledge about what they do and do not like in terms of things like activities and toys, clothes, food, and other people. Toddlers need to be able to make choices that allow them to assert their preferences. Although they are still discoverers, they are now ready and able to go where they want—and sometimes where you *do not* want them to go! Likewise, they still need to feel secure. As toddlers try new things, they will frequently come back for a quick hug or check in with their eyes to make sure you are watching them.

Things to Hide and Find

In toddlerhood, most children are one step closer to understanding true object permanence—the understanding that even though something disappears from sight, it continues to exist. They can now search for something that is completely out of sight, but only if they have seen where it was hidden or they have witnessed where it disappeared (e.g., under the couch or table). And toddlers do really enjoy looking for and finding hidden objects! You can take advantage of this interest to create fun experiences for toddlers that support their emerging understanding of object permanence and help build their attention span. Sensory tables and sandboxes are perfect for hiding and finding things.

Any small object will do in this type of play, but toddlers love small toys that fit in their hands, such as molded plastic animals. As you play with toddlers at the sensory table or sandbox, make sure they see you take one of the toys and bury it under the sand or whatever material is in the sensory table that day. Although toddlers rarely need encouragement to go after a hidden toy, you may need to prompt them ("Oh! What happened to the horse? Where did it go?"). Toddlers understand that when something disappears, it continues to exist, but they may not try to find it unless they have observed where it was hidden or placed.

Ideas for Supporting Focused Attention

- Give children choices and experiment to find materials that are motivating and interesting to them.

- Avoid offering too many choices, which can be confusing and distracting.

- If a child is playing alone, be patient and give them time and space without intruding.

- If a child is sharing an experience with you, engage in joint attention and soft, encouraging conversation to draw out the experience.

Finger Paints

Toddlers love messy play. Finger painting is a wonderfully fun activity for toddlers—although not always as much fun for those who have to clean up after it! Finger painting is an excellent sensory integration experience, as it stimulates multiple senses at once. It is certainly a tactile experience, involving the fingers, hands, and often the whole lower arms of toddlers. Toddlers enjoy seeing the patterns, lines, and shapes that can be made as they trace their fingers and hands through the material. Finger painting can be done with a variety of substances, including colorful nontoxic foams and edible paint. Although these things will not harm toddlers, make sure they do not taste or eat large quantities to prevent them from getting sick. This is particularly true if any additional substances, such as sand, have been added to give the material texture.

At this age, toddlers begin to understand that different objects have different purposes. They can learn the difference between food and nonfood items, but you must remain diligent and patient. This often requires direct instruction to be given, such as "Not in your mouth, please. Yucky. This is not food." For this reason, we recommend not using food items for play materials because it can cause confusion. It is hard to explain to a toddler that today we cannot taste the finger paint, when a few days before, pudding was used as paint and it was okay to taste it! It is also critical to consider that many families face food insecurity; by avoiding the use of food items in play, you instill in children the concept of respecting food as a valuable source of nutrition.

Although most toddlers love messy play, there are exceptions. You may encounter toddlers who really do not like having dirty hands or the feel of certain textures, like those found in many finger-painting activities. This may be, in part, due to temperament, or it may be about what they like and dislike. This is not necessarily a sign that there is anything wrong in terms of the child's sensory integration but rather a challenge for you to find sensory experiences that the child does like.

Twos (Identity Seekers)

You know it when you see it—2-year-olds just look and seem different from toddlers. Physically, their bodies are longer and leaner, and this, along with their more mature depth perception and hand–eye coordination, allows them to walk and run with more grace and confidence. Their ability to talk is developing at an astounding rate, and they have a strong and growing sense of who they are and who their family members are and an idea about the things that make them different from the other children in their group. Toddlers can pay attention for several minutes to something that interests them and sit attentively as you read their favorite books. In addition, twos can carry out their own experiments as they seek answers to spoken and unspoken questions of what, why, and how things and people are the way they are.

Hidden Things to Discover

Sensory tables and tubs offer good experiences for most of the birth-to-3 period and beyond. For 2-year-olds, however, they provide a way for you to observe just when they understand object permanence. As Xu (2013) described, "the infant's starting point is vastly different from what we see later in development, and much constructive learning is needed to get to the more mature concept" (167). For children to learn true object permanence during their first two years of life, they must actively explore the world using all of their senses. This is best supported by experiences with objects and people in their environment during unhindered free play.

To see if the 2-year-olds you are playing with have learned object permanence, bury some objects in the material in the sensory table or in the sandbox outdoors when the children are not looking. Again, small toys like molded plastic animals are good for this. Gather the twos around you and ask them to find the buried treasure. For instance, name a favorite object and ask them, "Can you find the green turtle? It's in the sand somewhere." The child has to remember the green turtle and hold it in their mind long enough to search and find it in a place they did not see it hidden or placed.

This same ability that allows 2-year-olds to look for missing objects makes them very good at recognizing when something is new and unexpected, as well as when something is missing or out of place in the environment. They may become upset by things they believe are not done correctly according to their keen sense of order. Maybe a toy is on the wrong shelf, someone's shoe is untied, or a visitor sings a favorite song differently than they are used to hearing it. They know where favorite things like toys and books are supposed to be and how things are supposed to look, and they will often react strongly when something is not as they expect. While this can become worrisome or annoying to adults around them, this behavior is actually a sign of cognitive growth related to moral development (coming to understand what is right and wrong) as well as aesthetic development (a sense of order and beauty) (Feeney & Moravcik 1987).

Tastes and Smells to Explore

Two-year-olds have highly developed senses of smell and taste that actually began in utero. However, while the sense of smell is remarkably well-developed at birth (Coleman 2020), the sense of taste in newborns is limited to being able to distinguish between sweet and sour—and preferring sweet! The senses of smell and taste work in tandem to define what we experience as flavor. Activities that involve the stimulation of smell and taste are natural and fun sensory integration experiences for twos. Such activities, by their nature, usually involve the senses of touch and sight as well. In addition, they provide opportunities to enrich vocabulary (e.g., *crispy* and *sweet* apples, *crunchy* carrots, *stinky* cheese, *yummy* or *yucky* asparagus) as they continue to sort out the properties of things in their worlds.

Smell jars, bottles, or small cups can be used to create opportunities to experience and experiment with smells. Again, like so many other play materials, these items can be found on the market. However, just as easily and usually more affordably, you can make them using directions suggested on numerous websites. Unbreakable bottles can be constructed (or purchased) so that when shaken, they release a scent; this can be independently explored by twos. Alternately, samples of different scents can simply be put in small unbreakable cups for an activity on the science table. Smells that are enjoyable and easily distinguished by 2-year-olds include those from scented extracts, like almond, vanilla, and peppermint, as well as from aromatic herbs and spices, such as rosemary, bay leaf, and garlic. Coffee grounds and powdered cocoa are fun to use as well. You can add pleasant smells, such as cinnamon, ginger, or natural lavender, to things like teacher-made playdough or whatever is used for finger painting so that children's sense of smell is stimulated during those activities along with touch and vision.

A fun and natural way to help twos experience and come to understand different flavors is through food preparation and cooking activities. (Remember: smell + taste = flavor.) Of course, you know this, but it bears repeating: always double check your list of ingredients for any food or sensory activity against any allergies that children have. Food preparation provides a wonderful means to support many areas of learning and development, but in the cognitive realm, it is particularly good for facilitating sensory integration, hand–eye coordination, focused attention, and patience, as well as early mathematics and science knowledge.

Music for Playing and Listening

The ability to process and remember music seems to be, like so many other cognitive capabilities, prewired in the brain before birth (Partanen et al. 2013). As Bryant (2014) puts it, "music is innate, universal, and part of the human experience from a very early age." The patterns and rhythms of music are so easily absorbed by young children's brains, helping their brains become faster and more efficient at transmitting signals, thus supporting learning. For instance, 2-year-olds who have been exposed regularly to music are found to have stronger early learning indicators for reading and mathematics (Geist, Geist, & Kuznik 2012; Lerner & Parlakian 2016).

Two-year-olds love to listen to music, dance to it, and sing to it, and they really love to make their own music! Because of all that, music can be used to create many enjoyable activities for supporting sensory integration and focused attention. Music and singing involve the sense of hearing, but when paired with movement or dance, vestibular and proprioceptive senses

integrate with hearing, firing brain cells in different parts of the brain and strengthening neural pathways. Similarly, these senses are stimulated when 2-year-olds play with safe, child-size musical instruments (e.g., simple bells, shakers, drums, triangles, tambourines).

Summary

Very young children use all of their senses to construct knowledge and understanding of the world around them, which is known as *sensorimotor learning*. Almost any experience is a sensory experience for children under age 3, but the toys and materials explored in this chapter specifically address three important cognitive developments and key learnings during this period: sensory stimulation and integration, object permanence, and focused attention.

Suggested Play Materials

- Beads to string

- Blocks to stack (e.g., wood, plastic, cloth)

- Boxes, baskets, carrier bags, and other containers to fill and empty

- Busy boards or boxes and activity cubes

- Feely bags and boxes

- Felt board with felt figures

- Grasping toys to hold, shake, and squeeze

- Lacing toys (e.g., cubes, boards, cards) or wooden shoes to practice lacing

- Links to hook or chain together

- Mobiles and baby play gyms

- Nesting cups

- Pegboards and pegs of different colors

- Pop (or snap-lock) beads

- Pounding or hammering toys, cobbler's benches, and xylophones

- Push toys (e.g., popcorn popper, lawn mower, vacuum cleaner)

- Puzzles with few pieces and knobs or handles

- Shape sorters of different types

- Simple games (e.g., guessing, matching)

- Small toys that fit in one hand (e.g., animals, vehicles)

- Sorting baskets or bowls

- Stacking rings

- Toys that respond with sound or visual effects

- Windup toys, hand-crank music boxes, and jacks-in-the-box

CHAPTER 6

Play Materials That Facilitate My Thinking and Problem-Solving Skills

For young children, quite literally, seeking explanations is as deeply rooted a drive as seeking food or water.

—Alison Gopnik, personal communication

Very young children use the knowledge and understanding they construct to think and problem solve. The best way for them to develop these important cognitive skills is through play that is meaningful and interesting to them. As Dewey ([1922] 2018) said, give children "something to do, not something to learn; the doing is of such a nature as to demand thinking, or the intentional noting of connection: learning naturally results" (98). Play materials can begin to support children's emerging ability to use working memory, understand cause and effect, change from trial-and-error problem solving to symbolic problem solving, and begin to match, sort, and recognize patterns. These experiences lead children to question what comes next, which is important in developing hypotheses and making predictions. It is also the question that keeps their mind curious, active, and engaged in its search for ways to explain things they encounter.

Young Infants (Security Seekers)

At birth, a young infant recognizes the sound of familiar voices, those they heard regularly during the last trimester of pregnancy. They are also born with a natural attraction to faces. Over time, they begin to distinguish between people and things that are familiar and those that are new. Their developing working memory allows them to begin to form expectations of how certain people and things will behave. Their understanding of cause and effect begins when a young infant first notices that some action or behavior on their part brings about a response in their environment or among the people around them and that the response happens the same way every time under the same circumstances (Gopnik 2009). For instance, a young infant may repeatedly drop a toy from their high chair in full expectation that an adult will pick it up.

Mobiles, Baby Play Gyms, and Other Hanging Things

One of the young infant's first discoveries is figuring out how to get their body to do what they want it to do, part of cause-and-effect learning and sensorimotor problem solving. Play materials that are particularly good to use with young infants include mobiles and things that hang down from a stand (sometimes called baby play gyms or activity mats), as well as toys that are designed to be attached to baby seats, strollers, and car seats. Very young infants will first randomly kick and flail their arms, simply enjoying the feel of the movement. After unexpectedly making contact with a toy that responds in a pleasing way and connecting with the toy randomly many more times, they eventually learn that they can control their bodies to bring about that enjoyable response whenever they wish!

This understanding leads to new experimentation with movements that are purposeful, as young infants kick, hit, grasp, or grab hold of all interesting objects in their view. Piaget said this all starts with what he called *primary circular reactions*, which involve a continuous looping, back and forth, between the body (movement) and recognition (cognition) centers of the brain (Bjorklund & Causey 2017). Provide plenty of safe and attractive objects within the young infant's reach for this important activity.

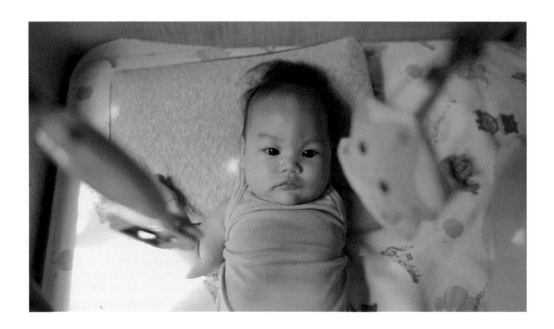

Busy Boxes and Activity Cubes

Young infants are incredibly keen observers who are typically very interested in what others are doing. By watching what is happening around them, they learn how to make things happen and how things work, and then they incorporate what they have learned into working memory. This occurs, for instance, when young infants repeatedly observe you flipping a light switch (cause) and then notice the room gets darker (effect). They watch as you wind up a toy dog using a key sticking out of its back and watch with interest as it walks across their high chair tray. These moments provide good opportunities for you to engage in joint attention and meaningful conversations with young infants. It is also the beginning of the child understanding that they can make things happen too. After the windup dog stops moving, they soon learn they can make sounds, smile, and move their bodies in such a way that you start it up again!

Classic busy boxes (or boards) and activity cubes are fun, interesting, and more reliable than electronic toys. There are many different variations of this toy available, but what most of them have in common is that they offer several different challenges for young infants to overcome in order to make things happen. For instance, the child might have to push a lever from side to side, turn a dial, push down on a large button, or flip open a small door in order to cause an effect, such as revealing an interesting image or producing a sound.

There are electronic versions of these toys that respond with sound or visual effects. Although we are not big supporters of electronic toys because we believe they may interfere with children's imaginations, there are several on the market that are fun and interesting to young infants. Such toys may light up, sing or play music, or even talk to young infants when they pat, slap, or touch them. These things do facilitate cause-and-effect learning, but be cautious on using battery-operated toys, which may lose power or break down easily and fail to work as expected, resulting in disappointing and possibly confusing young learners.

Mobile Infants (Discovery Seekers)

You will observe young infants' ever-increasing ability to use working memory as they become mobile. For instance, they become very good at reading cues in the environment (e.g., your movements and behaviors) and using them to anticipate daily routines. It is not uncommon to see mobile infants crawl or cruise over to the eating area in anticipation of lunch or snack being served when they see you begin to clean up the books and toys. Similarly, they know it is time to move toward the door to go outside when they see you getting out the sunscreen. Be observant and you will also see mobile infants begin to match things that go with one another, like putting a toy bottle in the mouth of a baby doll or finding another child's pacifier on the carpet and giving it back to that child.

Nesting Cups, Stacking Rings, and Small Blocks

There are many classic toys that allow mobile infants to practice their budding ability to match objects. Nesting cups (or bowls) of one type or another have been a staple for generations. They do just what they say, a small cup nests inside a big one, then one even smaller within the first one, and so on. No more than three cups are reasonable to use with mobile infants. At a glance, nesting cups seem like a very simple toy, but they offer numerous opportunities for discovery and problem-solving challenges for children. Once the cups are separated, they only fit back together one way. They can be inverted and stacked one upon another to build small towers, two to three cups high, or with two on the bottom and one on the top. The cups can be used for pouring and scooping water and other materials or as molds to press down on sand or playdough.

Another classic toy that offers similar challenges as nesting cups are stacking rings. This popular toy consists of a base with a plastic, wood, or cloth cone of graduated-size and differently colored rings that fit one over the other, starting with the biggest at the base and getting progressively smaller as more are added. As with nesting cups, offer no more than three rings at this age. With encouragement at first, mobile infants can take the rings off one at a time and learn to put them back in order.

Similar activities can be done with blocks. Again, it is best to start with no more than three until the child can easily and reliably stack three blocks. Any number of different types of small blocks available on the market will work, as long as they can easily be held by a mobile infant and do not wobble when stacked. One such version is the classic square, wooden, primary-colored blocks featuring letters and numbers on their faces. Mobile infants often either line the blocks up side by side or stack them, first two blocks high and then three. Learning how to balance objects is a major development, requiring coordination of body and mind acting together. Soon, they will be constructing more complex block structures. By their third birthday, most children are able to stack up to nine blocks and build simple block structures using three to four blocks.

Nesting cups, stacking rings, and small blocks are all good for working on *sequencing*—understanding what comes next—and for learning and practicing perceptual skills with colors, sizes, shapes, relative positions, and how things fit together. As the children play, you can name the colors of the toys or use words and phrases like *add one more, first, last, big, bigger*, and *biggest* to describe them. While engaging in joint attention, count the cups, rings, or blocks.

Boxes, Baskets, and Carrier Bags

Mobile infants love, love, love dumping things out of containers! Some enjoy putting things in containers as well, but there is something that is just so very satisfying about emptying things out of bags, baskets, boxes, big woven carrier bags, purses, and more. These are not expensive play materials to have in the child care setting. Use almost any kind of safe container you can find, as long as mobile infants can easily use it. They understand that a container can hold things—often very interesting things—and that while in the container, these things are not visible. Emptying the container (cause) brings about delightful discovery of what is inside (effect). Remember, at this age, object permanence is not fully developed, meaning infants do not yet understand that an object exists when it is out of their sight, so every new reveal can fascinate and delight children. When the mobile infant gets closer to the toddler period, they will enjoy putting things into containers as well.

Toddlers (Autonomy Seekers)

The continuing development of working memory, understanding of cause and effect, and budding abilities to match and sort all seem to come together for toddlers. Toddlers now have memory of certain key characteristics of the different people in their lives, the usual location of objects in their environments (e.g., toys, books, furniture), and all the steps usually taken in a routine activity (e.g., "After we clean up, we wash our hands, go to the table, and then we eat"). These capabilities allow toddlers to understand different qualities of objects, as well as people, and they can now separate items into two piles or categories (e.g., toy kittens versus puppies, blue things versus red things, cookies versus broccoli). Although they mostly engage in trial-and-error problem solving, they can also now observe how others solve problems and imitate that behavior.

Toddlers are focused on autonomy and very much want to be able to do things on their own. At the same time, although they are becoming more persistent about working on something even if it is difficult, they are easily frustrated. This combination often results in strong emotional responses. Supply plenty of play materials that offer interesting challenges but also offer ways for toddlers to feel successful on their own with little or no adult intervention.

Pegboards and Pop Beads

Toys such as pegboards and pop (or snap-lock) beads are useful for developing an understanding of sequencing. In addition, you can use these materials to help toddlers develop early pattern recognition (e.g., "Look! We have a red one, and a blue one, and another red one, and another blue one"). Pop beads come in multiple bright colors and are just the right size for toddlers' hands. They make a satisfying *pop* when taken apart and a *snap* when successfully put together. It is also not that easy to do, and at first presents quite a challenge to toddlers. Similarly, it takes some effort to get the brightly colored wooden or plastic pegs to go into a pegboard, but many toddlers enjoy the effort. It is good for you to be nearby and provide support as needed to keep toddlers from becoming overly frustrated and giving up too soon. When toddlers are persistent and they finally are successful (with or without your direct assistance), they feel a sense of satisfaction and accomplishment.

Puzzles

Puzzles are important because they help children work on spatial recognition and orientation of objects, important thinking and problem-solving skills. While most mobile infants enjoy dumping the pieces of a puzzle out on the floor or table and then motoring away, toddlers are ready and interested in putting puzzles together. We recommend very simple puzzles made of wood or heavy, thick cardboard and with knobs or handles that are comfortably sized for toddlers to grasp. In general, toddlers are not ready for puzzles that have interlocking pieces that come together to make a whole image. Rather, provide puzzles in a plain frame that holds no more than two to four knobbed pieces. Each piece should constitute an entire object such as a full image of a butterfly or a cow, which would then fit easily into a butterfly or cow cutout on the puzzle frame.

Twos (Identity Seekers)

The working memory of 2-year-olds is developed to the point that most of them are able to talk about or even act out—at least in a simple way—something that happened in the past. You can actually see memory in action when you watch twos engage in pretend play. Much of what you observe is their imitation of something they experienced or observed. Their improved working memory and more mature understanding of cause and effect allows them to make predictions about what will happen and reflect on what caused something to happen (e.g., that block tower fell down because I made it too tall).

Sometime between the ages of about 2 and 2½, children develop the ability to hold images in their minds (called *mental images*) long enough to think about something before physically acting on it. They also begin to have private thoughts. Before this time, because thought and action happened at the same moment, you could "see" what younger 2-year-olds were thinking:

> "You can *see* toddlers thinking," my child development professor told our graduate school class. I nodded and thought to myself, how right he is. I pictured my then [almost] 2-year-old son running full tilt across the room that afternoon with a gleam in his eye toward a full plate of cookies on the counter. I remembered the night before when he sat on the floor with a shape sorter and how his furrowed brow and frustrated expression became a look of insight and then delight as he figured out how to fit the funny octagonal-shaped piece into the right slot. Any of us who have parented infants and toddlers or who have been their teachers can think of many examples of this phenomenon of "seeing" toddlers think. (McMullen 1998, 65)

Being able to think symbolically using mental images is an amazing developmental step because it allows children to think through a series of actions that they might use to solve a problem. In essence, their minds are processing "I will need to do this and then this for this thing to work."

Matching Games and Shape Sorters

Being able to categorize (identify how things are alike and different), sort (separate things that are alike from those that are different), and organize (put like things into piles or containers that hold only things that are alike) are important precursor skills that prepare children for reading and mathematics. Two-year-olds can sort things into multiple piles or groups, although they sort by only one attribute (e.g., shape, texture, type of object, length) at a time. The first attribute they usually sort by is color. Twos usually start doing this on their own and need little if any encouragement to do it. They seem to crave order and control over things in their world, and this activity helps fill that need.

Matching games can be purchased, but they can also be created by the teacher. Many materials work well for this, such as using a felt board and felt figures or a magnetic whiteboard and magnets to create simple matching challenges. An easy-to-make classic matching game is a simplified version of the card game Memory, using cardboard or heavy paper to make oversized laminated picture cards that show images familiar to the children. To begin, use no more than three to four individual images, which can be matched in terms of one attribute (e.g., by the color red, by the fact they are all dogs). Create two cards for each image, making a total of no more than six or eight cards. The cards should be laid out face up on a table (or on a felt or magnet board) in front of a 2-year-old or a small group. Encourage them to find, for instance, the two yellow ducks, the two blue flowers, or the two red balls. They will soon catch on and be able to do it on their own. Before you know it, they will be capable of playing with a larger deck of cards to sort and match.

Shape sorters work on the same cognitive skills. Many forms of the classic shape-sorter toy exist. Most comprise of a main body, or container, that is either a plastic or wooden sphere or cube that can be opened up. The container has a number of holes or openings, each in a specific shape (such as a circle, square, triangle, octagon, and star), and comes with chunky pieces in corresponding shapes that can only fit in the appropriate opening. In other words, the round piece will only fit in the round opening, the square piece only in the square opening, and so on. This is a self-correcting toy because it will work one and only one way—each piece has only one hole that will match it. You can observe which of the twos in the group playing with the shape sorter pick up a piece and randomly try it in differently shaped holes until they get it to work (trial-and-error problem solvers) and which twos look at each piece and then spend a moment or two trying to figure out which hole they think matches before testing their solution (symbolic problem solvers).

Guessing Games and Feely Boxes

Guessing games help 2-year-olds develop the cognitive skills of hypothesizing and predicting. Just showing them a bag or box with something in it and asking what they think is inside it can elicit great excitement with a lot of ideas being thrown out. An added dimension to this game comes with the use of feely bags or boxes. These containers are mostly closed but allow children to stick their hands inside, grasp hold of an object, and guess what they are holding using only their sense of touch. This activity requires a 2-year-old to be able to retrieve some kind of mental image or sense of the object using working memory and sensorimotor understanding to figure out what it is. You then ask them to make a guess (hypothesis) and test it by pulling their hand and the object out of the bag or box.

Your Role as Teacher

- Provide play materials that spark children's curiosity and interest
- Allow freedom of exploration and experimentation
- Encourage children by using a positive tone of voice and words
- Help only when necessary (e.g., by scaffolding, reorienting a toy, asking open-ended questions)
- Model and provide opportunities for children to practice making hypotheses and predictions

Summary

Increasingly sophisticated skills related to thinking and problem solving emerge through the first three years. These skills help the very young child solve problems, such as getting your attention to tell you they're ready to get out of their crib, finding a temporarily lost toy, or figuring out which button to push to make music. Providing challenges for very young children to solve is important to inspiring learning because "when they are successful [at problem solving], children feel confident and proud, which motivates them to explore and learn more from the people and world around them" (Zero to Three 2010b).

Suggested Play Materials

- Baby dolls and accessories (e.g., carriages, clothes, cribs)
- Bead mazes and abacuses
- Beanbags in different shapes or with letters or numbers
- Binoculars and magnifying glasses
- Blocks in a variety of sizes and materials
- Cloth books, including those with interactive features (e.g., lift the flap, mirrors, touch and feel)
- Letter and number stamps that use washable ink
- Loose parts for projects
- Magnets in different shapes and sizes (e.g., numbers, letters)
- Materials with buttons, buckles, and snaps
- Molded plastic animals (e.g., birds, bugs, dinosaurs, farm animals, mothers and babies, sea creatures)
- Molded plastic people reflecting different ages, ethnicities, and genders, including male, female, and nongender specific
- Noncompetitive games (e.g., giant dice, dominoes, magnetic fish, beanbags with numbers and letters, cloth bowling balls and pins, things to count and sort)
- Paper, cardboard pieces and tubes, and PVC pipes and connectors
- Playdough and clay
- Playsets (e.g., farm, house, playground)
- Sand toys (e.g., rakes, shovels, buckets, molds, vehicles)
- Simple matching games (e.g., egg shape sorter)
- Stuffed animals and plush toys that respond to touch with sound (e.g., crinkle, beep, squeak)
- Vehicles with wheels to push, pull, or ride on
- Water toys (e.g., things that float, funnels, colanders, sprinklers, waterwheels)
- Wooden puzzles with letters, numbers, and shapes

CHAPTER 7

Play Materials That Inspire My Approaches to Learning

What motivates infant play is the pure joy of mastering objects and actions; play is viewed not as a means to an end but as an end itself.

—Jeesun Jung and Susan Recchia, "Scaffolding Infants' Play Through Empowering and Individualizing Teaching Practices," *Early Education and Development*

Cognitive learning and development, as presented in Chapters 5 and 6, involve the acquisition of knowledge and understanding about the world and how it works, as well as the skills to think and problem solve. That is not all, however; there's more to the process of development and learning than just collecting more and more knowledge and developing better, more efficient skills. In order to keep moving forward—to be educated—everyone, including very young children, must have a belief that *they can learn* and that *learning is valuable* to them in some way. They must be motivated! They must be inspired!

These beliefs (or dispositions) for learning support various *approaches to learning*, or in other words, how children learn and how they feel about learning (Hyson 2008; Hyson & Douglas 2019). You will notice children have different ways in which they approach learning; they might be cautious or take risks, be persistent or give up easily, be open to new ideas or not. This is sometimes described as *executive function*, which is how a child manages their thinking to reach their goals and face challenges (Munakata et al. 2013), and it is related to imagination and creativity—that is, being able to design and make something original (e.g., structures, art, music, dramatic plays) or imagine different possibilities and outcomes to solve problems (Suddendorf & Fletcher-Flinn 2011; Vygotsky 2004). In this chapter, we consider how to build on very young children's natural love of learning and support the development of positive approaches to learning that will last a lifetime.

Young Infants (Security Seekers)

When you support young infants and help them feel safe and secure, they approach learning with openness to and interest in the world around them. Their sense of trust in caring adults makes them more willing to try new things and continue exploring and learning. Young infants show particular interest in things that are new to them, so play materials should be familiar enough to foster security but novel enough that they are attractive, interesting, and motivating. Young infants will tell you when they are excited and engaged by rewarding you with smiles and laughter. (There's nothing better than eliciting a good belly laugh from a young infant!)

Cloth Books

Cloth books bring much enjoyment to young infants. Bright and contrasting colors of well-designed cloth books grab and hold young infants' attention. The different features on each page bring new things to discover and experience. The best cloth books have simple images with highly contrasting colors that seem to pop off the pages. Some have different textures—soft, smooth, rough, scratchy, sticky—that support the sensorimotor exploration discussed in Chapter 5. They may also include special features like peekaboo flaps or mirrors, and some may even make sounds as the child interacts with them. Others have handles so young infants can easily grab, shake, and wave them about.

Add new cloth books with different or novel features to your collection to keep the young infants interested. Whenever rotating in new toys or books, be sure to keep those that are highly popular or especially beloved by certain children. When security and trustworthiness are such urgent needs for young children especially, predictability and stability are very important. It is a delicate but important balancing act between providing a sufficient number of new and interesting things and making sure that each child feels comfortable by having the things they love reliably present.

Cloth books can be purchased or handmade by teachers, families, or others who are particularly creative and proficient in sewing. Whatever the source, make sure that the books are sturdy and safe, with no small loose pieces, and that they can be washed easily.

Plush Toys

Like cloth books, stuffed animals are a favorite of young infants. Both nurture the teacher–child relationship as you explore them one-on-one with an infant held securely on your lap. Joint attention and important conversations are shared during such quiet activities. When an infant shows interest in a stuffed animal, it is natural to comment and engage them in conversation ("Oh! What does the lion say, Tommy? *Roarrrrr.* That's right."). Young infants are just beginning to discriminate between objects and benefit from hearing the names of creatures and learning the different sounds they make. Some toys even make their own satisfying responsive sounds (e.g., crinkle, beep, jingle, squeak) as young infants explore them on their own.

Large plush hand puppets are similarly open ended and used by many teachers to prompt the attention of young infants and elicit responses like small vocalizations, smiles, and laughter. You can use them as props as you sing songs and tell stories or simply to make infants feel happy and joyful. "Puppets are singular in their diverse ability to entertain, teach, and connect" (Marinovich 2016).

Mobile Infants (Discovery Seekers)

Mobile infants approach new discoveries with keen interest and curiosity. Their growing attention span allows them to listen longer to stories and songs, look at objects more closely, and spend more time manipulating and experimenting with those objects. At the same time that mobile infants are moving about more easily in their play environments, they are also developing impulse control. *Impulse control* is an executive function that keeps them from doing something they should not do. For example, they are learning to stop themselves from touching things that might hurt them, like electrical outlets or cords hanging from a fan or music player. They are also learning to ask you (through gestures, vocalizations, and so on) to get them what they need or want, rather than, for example, climbing up on a shelf they have been warned not to climb. Mobile infants should be supplied with numerous safe open-ended materials that capitalize on their love of discovery and need for activity.

Bead Mazes

A classic toy that comes in an endless variety of shapes, sizes, and configurations is the bead maze. Bead mazes consist of a wooden or heavy plastic base that anchors both ends of one or more sturdy primary-colored wires that curve, dip, and turn in various ways from beginning to end. Running along the wires are wooden or plastic beads in a variety of shapes, usually including spheres and square blocks that spin and glide along the wire pathways. Bead mazes have no loose pieces and, as long as they are well made, are very safe for mobile infants to play with on their own. Some bead mazes are small and come with suction cups for easy use on tabletops or high chair trays; others are large, relatively stable structures meant for floor play. Still others are very large and are built into tables.

There are so many benefits associated with playing with bead mazes. Multiple cognitive development and learning areas are touched on in some way too when using this simple toy. The different colors, ability to move objects easily across the wires—up and down, back and forth—and even the rather pleasant clacking sound of the beads hitting the base of the maze make it a sensory stimulation and integration activity. Depending on their size and complexity, bead mazes allow children to match, sort, and create patterns with the beads using sensorimotor trial-and-error exploration, which promotes hand–eye coordination and spatial perception while offering endless fun and fascination.

Important foundations for later learning are also addressed when you and mobile infants play with bead mazes. For example, simple activities such as moving one bead along the maze as you say, "One," and then moving another bead to join it as you say, "Two," and so on starts forming the concepts of one-to-one correspondence. Mobile infants start hearing the words associated with cardinal numbers (e.g., *one, two, three*), and you provide language for relative, or ordinal, position (e.g., *first, second, last*). A closely related toy that provides many of the same opportunities for sorting, making patterns, and counting is the children's abacus.

Sand and Water

"Sand or water must be available to the children each day," stated Vanover (2018). *Must*, she said—and we certainly agree. As soon as a young infant becomes mobile and can crawl or make their way to the sensory table and pull themselves up to stand along the edge, there should be sand, water, or some similar material in it for them to explore. Sand and water play is an open-ended activity that can occur outdoors as well, with mobile infants sitting inside or alongside the edge of the sandbox, splashing in a wading pool (under careful supervision), or getting splashed by a sprinkler.

Sand and water play is highly motivating, and it supports (Vanover 2018)

> Imagination and creativity

> Important approaches to learning, including persistence and curiosity

> Development of language and communication, mathematics, and science skills

When mobile infants fill small cups or bowls with sand or water, they construct an understanding of concepts such as *full* and *empty* and start forming ideas about volume. They learn about the basic properties of water and sand, how water makes their hands wet, and how it flows and splashes as they pour it. Children also discover that, although they can pour sand out of a container in the same way as water, it feels and behaves very differently.

You can supply different types of sand and water toys, keeping some back to add in or swap out with the current ones when interest starts to wane or you see the children are ready for a new challenge. Some of the toys most suitable at this age for sand and water play are things most mobile infants will be able to manipulate easily with their hands, such as cups or small containers, large spoons or small shovels, buckets, and strainers or colanders, as well as simple waterwheels. Things like rubber ducks and floating plastic fish are fun to put in a water table, and mobile infants love to discover molded plastic animals buried in the sand.

Toddlers (Autonomy Seekers)

Toddlers are becoming more persistent in their efforts as they play and work, and, of course, they really like to do things themselves. One thing that inspires their dispositions for learning and fires their imagination is pretend play. Although toddlers are still pre-symbolic thinkers and most do not yet engage in dramatic play with other children, they do engage in pretend play based on familiar activities, and they show *deferred imitation*, meaning they imitate things in their play that they have seen others do. Even though they will occasionally use one thing to substitute another—such as a rectangular block to represent a phone—when supporting pretend play, it is best to provide realistic props. Toddlers should be given plenty of uninterrupted time for free play to exercise their need for independence.

Playsets

Toddlers enjoy playing with toy props that represent familiar or interesting scenes that they can control easily. Playsets usually include wooden or hard molded plastic structures that represent something that may be familiar, such as a farm, house, playground, grocery store, restaurant, or campground. A number of figurines are sold with or can be added to playsets, like animals, plants, people, and vehicles. Playsets are wonderful for sparking toddler imagination, and their open-ended nature inspires creativity as the child envisions new and different scenarios for the inhabitants of the scenes.

As toddlers become more sophisticated in pretend play, they understand more and more that certain things represent other things. They may come to see, for instance, that the playset grocery store is a lot like the store on their block or that the camping scene is like what they sometimes do as a family. Furthermore, children begin to see themselves in the scenes and create stories about them. They realize that they can be anything or anyone that they want! This is the advent of *dramatic play*, play in which the child puts themselves in an imaginary context and acts out a role.

Baby Dolls

Playing with baby dolls and acting out what they have seen others do with babies is a familiar and comforting pretend play for toddlers, one that may keep their imaginations and interest engaged for relatively long periods of time. For this type of play, provide washable plastic or cloth baby dolls that can easily be held and cradled in the arms of toddlers. The dolls should represent multiple ethnicities (including, at least, Asian, Black, Brown, and White babies),

whether or not all of this diversity is represented in the setting's children and families at the time (NAEYC 2019a). If affordable, diapers and changes of clothes that fit the baby dolls are nice to have, as are other accessories, such as bottles, a stroller, a high chair, and a crib or cradle.

Toddlers enjoy engaging with small groups of peers for activities such as baby washing. They love giving their babies a bath and will do this companionably alongside their peers under your guidance, persisting in the activity for relatively long periods of time. Such an activity encourages toddlers to follow a multistep sequence that may involve any number of activities, such as washing and drying the baby, diapering and clothing it, feeding it, and then putting it down for a nap or taking it for a stroller ride. Manipulating objects to create different scenarios demonstrates a leap in cognitive and intellectual capability and allows you to see how toddlers are processing information in the world around them.

Twos (Identity Seekers)

Compared to toddlers, 2-year-olds are more comfortable doing things that have multiple steps and greater complexity. Although their pretend play is still based on familiar, everyday themes, as their play becomes more symbolic, you will see twos engage in some planning, thinking a couple of steps ahead about what they need in their play. In fact, many teachers may see an interesting new behavior emerge: twos talking quietly to themselves as they plan and engage in play, such as when they work through challenges like puzzles or create something new. This is something Vygotsky (1987) called *private speech*. Private speech is positively related to staying on task and persistence (Davis, Meins, & Fernyhough 2013). You may also notice that some twos talk to imaginary friends. This is not worrisome but rather a sign of a strong imagination and creative tendencies (Murkoff 2019).

Noncompetitive Games

Games can be useful in supporting important approaches to learning in 2-year-olds, including a willingness to take risks, enjoy a challenge, work toward a goal, learn to be strategic, and plan ahead. In addition, games help 2-year-olds work on executive function skills (e.g., maintaining attention, being patient, persisting). They also offer a way for you to observe different children's approaches to learning. Perhaps most importantly, games support positive dispositions toward learning because games are fun! (Or at least, they are meant to be.) Remember the connection between strong emotions—preferably strongly positive ones—and learning. Although you have certain learning goals in mind when you set up games for 2-year-olds to play, children should never feel forced to play a game. If they do, it is no longer play, and they may not get the full developmental and learning benefit from the activity that they could.

Two-year-olds are not ready for games with complicated rules or that are competitive when someone wins and someone loses. That said, there are many appropriate and fun games that you can create for 2-year-olds. Although these examples can be purchased, there are many fun games that you can craft out of generally available, inexpensive materials.

Oversized dominoes, large soft blocks with numbers and dots (e.g., one dot and the numeral 1, two dots and the numeral 2), rubber ducks that have numbers painted on their undersides, and lettered bowling pins are all examples of play materials that can be used to create noncompetitive games that are fun and encourage positive dispositions for learning. Begin by using materials that represent nothing higher than three to start with; as a child needs more challenge, no higher than five (i.e., no more than three to five bowling pins, dominoes with no more than three to five dots, no more than three to five rubber ducks). Fun and challenging games include

> **Fishing.** Set rubber ducks with numbers painted on their undersides floating in a tub of water. Have children use a net to fish for rubber ducks; alternately, attach magnets to the ducks and have the children use a fishing string with a magnet on the end. The children can name the number on the bottom of ducks that they catch, or you can help them count how many ducks in total they caught. You can also challenge them to catch three ducks.

> **Bowling.** Set up cloth bowling pins and have children count aloud the number of pins that they are able to knock down ("One, two, three bowling pins!"). You can also have the children knock down numbered bowling pins and tell you what number was on the pin.

> **Dominoes.** Play a simple game of dominoes with twos by showing them how to match the number of dots on one domino with those on another domino, emphasizing that one player goes first, another player goes second, and so on.

> **Dice.** Ask children to take turns throwing jumbo-size cloth or wooden dice and have them tell you how many dots appear on the top. When they need more of a challenge, play with them and ask, "Is your number bigger (or smaller) than mine?"

Infants and Toddlers at Play

Two-year-olds are working on strengthening their natural intuition for mathematics, which began developing at 4 to 6 months (Jung, Kloosterman, & McMullen 2007; Starr, Libertus, & Brannon 2013). Games such as these help children learn to instantaneously recognize and understand quantities of number, an important part of number sense. This aspect of understanding quantity occurs when children are able to internalize, or have a sense of, for instance, "threeness," "fiveness," and so on. It involves understanding a number so well that it is instantly known without having to think about it when it is seen represented in some way (e.g., three dots, three ducks, the numeral 3). For an adult, this is the same concept as having a sense of six feet. If you hear that someone is six feet tall, you have a deep-down understanding of what that means and about how tall they will appear when you see them.

Project Materials

Working on longer-term projects is a wonderful and fun way to excite very young learners, tap into their imaginations, and build confidence in their ability to create (LeeKeenan & Edwards 1992). Doing projects with 2-year-olds encourages them to work and play with others, and it nurtures the cognitive skills related to approaches to learning, including planning, representation, and reflection, as well as imagination and creativity (Wanerman 2013). Projects begin when a topic emerges naturally from children's curiosity or something you notice is an interest in your setting. This work takes many forms, including

> **Construction:** making something (e.g., turning a large cardboard box into a truck, using PVC pipes to make water flow in a specific direction, building a ramp for toy cars on the playground)

> **Inquiries:** learning about things they are interested in (e.g., what squirrels like to eat, where babies come from)

> **Displays:** creating an artistic display to make an art gallery or give as a special gift for someone in the community

Projects are meant to be planned, documented, displayed, celebrated, and, in the end, reflected upon in some way (Helm & Katz 2016; Kogan & Pin 2009).

Consider what resources children will need to explore their topic and represent what they are learning. Props and open-ended materials like loose parts allow children agency to design meaningful play. "Loose parts are materials that can be moved, carried, combined, redesigned, lined up, and taken apart and put back together in multiple ways. [They] can be used alone or combined with other materials" (Better Kid Care 2019). There are a number of toys, materials, and resources you can provide to support projects, including the following:

> Binoculars and magnifying glasses to examine things

> Containers for collecting things

> Art materials such as paint, markers, and paper

> Playdough and clay to represent and document what they are learning

> Materials and loose parts to build large three-dimensional displays of their work and creations, such as cardboard boxes and tubes and PVC pipes and connectors

> Props for pretend play to aid in the telling of the story of the work

Project work creates a sense of shared ownership in a group and a sense of pride that inspires future learning. Documentation of the process is helpful information for you to communicate to families about the development of their 2-year-olds, particularly in terms of the quality of their thinking and what they have been learning (Helm & Katz 2016).

Summary

In this chapter, we considered play materials that support positive approaches to and the joy of learning. Very young children have a natural love of learning that needs to be supported so they will value and enjoy learning for the rest of their lives. As Kohn (2004) stated, "To be well-educated is to have the desire as well as the means to make sure that learning never ends" (10).

In Your Words

Ellen Veselack, director of the preschool program and associate director for the Outdoor Classroom Project at the Child Educational Center in La Cañada, California, provides the reflection below about supporting cognitive development, learning, and well-being in very young children.

....

At the Child Educational Center, we have a strong focus on our outdoor classrooms, and we take even the very youngest children outdoors on a daily basis. There is no better way for children to gain important cognitive skills, including executive function skills, than in a nature-filled space. We have very little in the way of plastic or manufactured materials in our infant and toddler spaces, indoors or outdoors. When children interact with the natural world—and the natural world is incorporated into many different spaces—they begin to understand a number of cognitive skills, such as spatial relationships, classification, a sense of quantity and size, geometry, cause and effect, and creativity and imagination.

All children, but especially very young infants, experience the world through their senses. They sense the elements around them aided by items such as wind chimes and spinners that come alive in a breeze. That same breeze rustles the leaves in the trees, provoking children to stare up into the branches. Birds twittering from a nearby branch create another provocation. Weather events, such as rain, offer opportunities not available indoors. The smell of the wet earth, the feel of the damp air, and the shimmer of the rain on the grass all give infants new information to process. Toddlers also love a good puddle for stomping in and mud to explore!

We carefully select natural materials that are safe for very young children to engage with and explore. Items such as stumps, logs, branches, leaves, pine cones, larger stones and shells, tree rounds, seedpods, and a variety of nontoxic plants all provide endless open-ended opportunities for infants and toddlers. These items become pretend food, telephones to talk on, or just items to fill baskets, boxes, and purses.

While much of our environment is full of nature, not everything can come from nature. There are the important three Bs of toys—books, baby dolls, and boxes. Books are everywhere for children, both indoors and out, and always available for children to pick out, pick up, look at by themselves, be read to, and even to explore orally (that is what young infants do, after all). Baby dolls are also important for children to role play and reenact family life. Infants and toddlers are drawn to baby dolls and already understand caring tenderly for them. They wrap them up in blankets, feed them with a pine cone bottle, and rock them to sleep. Toddlers, in particular, have a great affinity for boxes. They climb in and out of them, pile into them together, and play hide-and-seek in them. They push them up and down the sidewalk. They fill them with leaves and then dump them out again.

A good rule of thumb for play materials for infants and toddlers is the less the toy does (minimal need for batteries, bells, and whistles), and the more natural it is, the richer the play will be.

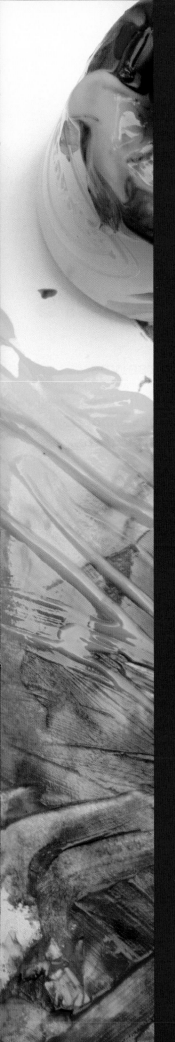

PART THREE

Social and Emotional Learning and Development

Suggested Play Materials

- Baby dolls
- Books for lap reading
- Carriers (e.g., totes, baskets, purses)
- Collaborative books and bookmaking
- Comfort items (e.g., blankets, plush animals)
- Family photos
- Home living area, equipment, and accessories
- Loose parts (and small objects) for easy carrying
- Mirrors
- Molded plastic or carved wooden animals and people
- Music (many types)
- Purposeful spaces (e.g., gathering space)
- Teachers, peers, and family members
- Vehicles that fit in one hand

CHAPTER 8

Play Materials That Help Me Understand Myself and Others

Through others, we become ourselves.

—Lev Vygotsky, *The Mind in Society: The Development of Higher Psychological Processes*

Children are born with an innate need to form relationships with others. Psychologist Lev Vygotsky ([1930–35] 1978, 1987) observed this need to connect with others in young children and described how they construct meaning from experiences within relationships. Play materials become a bridge for connecting with others through shared experiences. These experiences define and deepen a child's relationship as a learner and their understanding of who they are as a person. Toys and other resources for play are important tools that weave these moments into lifelong patterns of learning. Your role is to select tools that relate to children's self-discovery and paths to building relationships.

We adopt the Vygotskian idea that all development and learning happen within a social context (Vygotsky [1930–35] 1978, 1987). With very young children, this means you nurture relationships between and among children and teachers and intentionally create spaces in which relationships can flourish. In this book, play materials include toys and resources as well as intangibles like scheduled time for play, one-on-one focused attention from a teacher, nurturing relationships, purposeful play spaces, and rich opportunities for diverse experiences. In this chapter on social and emotional learning and development, the intangible resources are as important—or often more important—than tangible play materials.

Young infants are primarily focused on security and highly dependent on the trusted adults in their lives to incorporate them into the routines and social engagement of the setting. Keeping this in mind, we acknowledge that above all, *you* are the most significant resource in your setting, particularly in nurturing children's social and emotional self-awareness.

Interactions and Relationships as Play Resources

You become a lifeline when young infants search for security, acting as a mirror to the child as they start to understand their emotional and social selves. You do this by reflecting back their emotions and giving words for and validation of their feelings. During playful interactions, young infants will look to you as a reference tool for how to respond, what emotions look like, and how to get more deeply in touch with their feelings. Through mindful and patient dialogue and modeling of appropriate responses, you allow young infants the space to become more attuned to their own needs and understanding of various situations (Lally 2008; Lally & Mangione 2006). This enables you to deepen your relationship with children, learn to meet each child *where* they are, and accept them for *who* they are.

You can reassure young infants by gazing into their eyes, describing their expressions of needs and emotions, and reassuring them verbally and with eye contact (even if you are across the room) that you will help them as soon as possible. Such actions validate the child's voice while also building a trusting relationship with them. Facial gazing and direct eye contact are crucial to security seekers as they begin to study the use of facial expression as a way to share their emotional experiences with others (Farzin, Hou, & Norcia 2012; LoBue 2016). You can further connect in such close and intimate moments by humming, singing songs, smiling, and talking softly.

Young infants use their bodies and early vocalizations, drawing you in to playing and talking with them, which are so important to early social and emotional learning. Security seekers quickly learn to use their bodies to express their personal needs (Driver 2011). A child may suck on their fingers to show they are ready for a bottle, rub their eyes to soothe their tired body and indicate they may need a nap, move their arms up and down quickly to show their dislike for a care routine or social situation, or smile, coo, and screech to get you to engage with them in a playful exchange. Young infants begin to experiment with how to express themselves through body language to convey their needs, curiosities, and sense of well-being. You will deepen the sense of trust between you and young infants by accepting the babbles, coos, cries, vocalizations, and body movements as true communications (Zero to Three 2016). Engage them in reassuring dialogue by responding with something like, "You're so frustrated. I hear you. It's going to be okay. Your milk is on the way," or "I see you! You look like you are ready to play!"

Comfort Items

Although young infants primarily seek out the social and emotional engagement found in secure attachment relationships, they also gain a deeper understanding of their emotional needs through play materials that foster self-soothing. When a young infant engages with comfort items such as soft blankets, plush animals, transitional objects (things that represent their home), and pacifiers, they begin constructing the building blocks of self-regulation (Gillespie 2015; McClelland & Tominey 2014).

As young infants snuggle into your embrace, they are warmed by your touch, and they feel the beat of your heart, the rhythm of your breathing, and the soothing sound of lullabies you sing or hum softly (Hewett 2013). You may also help a group of young infants feel peaceful and comfortable by sitting in front of them and taking time to engage with each child while also addressing the group collectively as a community (Feierabend 2019).

Music can create wonderful moments of bonding. During care routines like giving a bottle or changing a diaper, sing familiar songs, such as ones that reflect the child's culture or language. Use a soft, soothing tone, and check the child's body language and facial expressions to see if you're connecting. Music can soothe sadness in young infants, create space to play with both speech and their bodies, and offer a reprieve from the sometimes overwhelming and overstimulating environment around them (Hewett 2013).

Mobile Infants (Discovery Seekers)

Because mobile infants need and are motivated by discovery, they venture forward, separating from the safety of their key attachment figures. Mobile infants begin to look more closely into the inner workings of their environment and experiment with building relationships independently. The suggested play materials encourage mobile infants to experiment with and engage in the thrill of discovering what their life has to offer.

Mirrors

Unbreakable mirrors provide endless possibilities for young children who are experimenting with independence and seeking new perspectives and opportunities to explore (Parks 2015). Whether it is a flexible mirror attached by Velcro to the floor or a sturdy mirror anchored to the wall, mobile infants will return to this play material repeatedly, experiencing a new type of self-discovery at each visit.

Mirrors help children begin the journey of understanding themselves as individuals and explore self-expression. Being able to view the background of their space and the people within it from this different vantage point, with their own body as the central focal point, offers a new avenue for discovery.

The child is fascinated by what they see, which you can encourage:

Gracie: (*Smiles and points at her image in the mirror.*)

Fran: You see the baby in the mirror? Yes! That's you, sweet girl. Smiling Gracie.

Gracie: (*Babbles and pats a palm repeatedly on part of the mirror reflecting the background.*)

Fran: Oh, yes, I see them too. Do you see your friends Anja and Joaquin? And Jane getting our lunch ready?

Although mobile infants do not fully recognize themselves in a mirror (not until about 18 months or so), mirror play facilitates the beginning of piecing together what it means to be a self, separate from peers and the environment.

Peers as Play Resources

Mobile infants are now able to engage with more physical ease as they turn their bodies and even crawl over to be near a friend or get a better perspective. Getting to know the intricacies of their own bodies, experimenting with eye contact, and observing others' reactions as they unfold provide a wealth of knowledge for the child's social and emotional self in a way that is initiated and controlled by the child.

Although mobile infants may now be able to understand that they are separate and different from the peer in front of them, they are not yet able to decipher that this is a separate person with thoughts and feelings that are different from their own. Play between mobile infants can be rather unpredictable. Stay close as young children engage with each other, providing a calm demeanor and meaningful strategies in the moment. A child with a high threshold for stimulation may reach out, exchange a toy, or babble back with excitement. Those who may need more support or have a higher sensitivity to stimulation may cry out and reach toward you when a peer gets too close. Allow children to engage from the safety of your lap as they work toward more independent play.

Mobile infants are at the very beginning of socializing and are thrilled to recognize that these other interesting beings in the environment respond in unique ways. Empathetic and compassionate care modeling becomes crucial as mobile infants develop prosocial play strategies, such as conflict resolution or recognizing when others want to play. Encounters with peers become increasingly important as mobile infants begin to find what experiences, materials, and people are the most meaningful to them and intentionally seek out those choices.

Toddlers (Autonomy Seekers)

Because toddlers have a growing sense of self as individuals and an even stronger desire to advocate for this new personhood in every way, they often seem quite emotional in play. Toddlers have a strong desire to make their own decisions, while they simultaneously crave boundaries. To address both needs, provide play materials that support growing independence and the need to experiment with power in a healthy and safe way. By doing so, you are facilitating their development of emotional self-regulation.

Small Objects and Carrying Totes

Support toddlers' child-initiated play with a learning environment that is easy to navigate and toys and materials that are accessible to all children in the group. Open-ended materials offer toddlers the ability to practice autonomy and decision-making in meaningful ways. Small objects such as plastic animals and people and loose parts become powerful tools for toddlers in their exploration of autonomy, particularly when paired with carrying totes or baskets (Karasik et al. 2012; Zorn 2012).

Toddlers like to load what they need into small baskets or totes that are just their size and carry them to another space. This activity frequently leads to social engagement or interaction as toddlers very much enjoy showing or sharing their collections with others, both peers and teachers. When children have the freedom to move play materials around within the learning environment, they develop confidence in their decision-making, as well as a sense of pride and ownership in the work they do.

Child-size totes and bags can also become prompts for one of the first and most-beloved types of toddler imaginative social play, which is imitating the goodbye routines of the familiar adults in their lives. Toddlers will often pack objects into small containers, move over to an exit door, and wave bye-bye. This type of imaginative play allows children to process how they feel during transitions, and it also allows them to experience a sense of power in situations over which they often have no control in their everyday lives.

Peers as Play Resources

Social engagement becomes even more intentional for toddlers as they begin to recognize the potential that lies within friendships. Deciding when you need to intervene and when to give some time and space to toddlers who are just beginning to interact with one another is often a difficult judgment call. Closely observe the children in play to gather more information about their play strategies and take note of areas that may need more direct guidance. You can support toddlers further in the moment by offering multiples of favorite play materials, positioning your body near collaborating peers, and keeping your expectations developmentally appropriate.

Position yourself close enough to step in and act as a calming presence for those moments that may become too physical (e.g., a child making one or more peers feel unsafe) or when one or more toddlers reach their limits emotionally. By supporting toddlers' needs and pausing to gather information before stepping in, you support children's individualized social and emotional learning and development.

Appropriate Expectations for Toddler–Peer Play

Most of you have seen, and probably chuckled knowingly, when you first read "A Toddler's Rules of Possession," a poem that has circulated online among families and educators alike ("If I like it, it's mine; If it's in my hand, it's mine; If I take it from you, it's mine . . ."). People find it funny because they have seen toddlers behave this way. Toddlers' new strong sense of self as individual, independent people has emerged, and along with it, they can be fiercely possessive of people and things. This is normal and it will not last forever. Do not expect toddlers to share willingly or to take turns; this is something learned over time through your encouragement and modeling. We recommend you have multiple copies of favorite toys and books, and please, be patient!

Staying near toddlers engaging in play with peers is always important! Sometimes toddler peer engagement may become highly energetic; taken to an extreme, it may become harmful to peers or even the materials in your environment. By staying close to the social play and remaining aware of their cues, you can redirect physical play toward safe alternatives. In this way, you help toddlers as they continue to gain mastery over their impulse control and regulate themselves emotionally. This may involve directing toddlers toward some other, more appropriate physical activity they may enjoy together, like rolling balls down a ramp on the climber. It might also mean modeling different methods for releasing excitement, such as jumping or clapping.

Infants and Toddlers at Play

Twos (Identity Seekers)

Two-year-olds begin to focus on *who* they are rather than just *how* they are, adding greater intention to early collaborative play found in toddlerhood. Imaginative play becomes an integral mechanism for twos to experience their own identity making. They are also ready to take on responsible roles, such as line leader, door holder, gardener (watering indoor plants), and fish feeder. Twos love having the chance to be helpful as they build a positive self-concept. The play materials discussed in the following sections allow space for creativity, more advanced collaborative play, and opportunities for the child to see themselves reflected in their work.

Collaborative Books

Collaborative bookmaking is an exciting process for expressive 2-year-olds. They can be involved throughout the process of construction from start to finish. Allow children the opportunity to pick a theme, assist in choosing (or even taking) photos, design and illustrate pages, and provide their own narration, which you can write down. This involvement fosters social skills while supporting the development of important emotional concepts, such as self-esteem, confidence, pride, and a strong sense of value in their capabilities. Embracing the involvement of each child as an individual allows everyone the space to express their own voice, while recognizing the contributions of others. Sharing the completed book nourishes notions of belonging within the community.

Collaborative books might depict, for instance, a cooking project, a glimpse into their neighborhood, a day in the life of your learning environment, a muddy walk outdoors, ways to care for friends, or a celebration of each child's family culture. These books become beloved additions to your setting's library, visited repeatedly as twos engage with them as concrete representations of shared experiences. This activity allows them to practice using their emerging social skills in collaborative storytelling as they look over photos, tell stories together, and point out new observations or hypotheses about experiences with peers.

Baby Dolls

Imaginative play allows 2-year-olds to experiment with different ways to resolve various emotional situations. When twos have the opportunity to dramatize power roles they experience with their care, they begin to practice their growing ability to view social experiences from multiple perspectives. Baby dolls become the perfect prop for this investigative and imaginative play.

Two-year-olds may recreate specific scenes, such as bathtime or feeding a baby, practicing the skills of nurturing and caring. They may use baby dolls as a means to enhance their emotional problem-solving abilities, giving voice and feeling to their doll and projecting their own empathy and emotion onto the doll. When you talk with twos about their doll play, use validating language. Highlight how the baby feels and what strategies the child is using to soothe their baby. Provide space that will allow twos room to create a caring environment in their play scene (Brooker 2016). Add a variety of props that are culturally, linguistically, and developmentally relevant to the children in your care, such as objects like or similar to those from the children's homes (NAEYC 2019a, 2020).

Baby dolls, much like any other play material, can be powerfully supportive as a child grows into themself, regardless of a child's gender identity. Empathy, relational problem solving, and well-practiced nurturing are important to all individuals throughout their lifetime.

Additional resources to include in your setting to support twos' strong sense of self are

> A **digital camera** for capturing children naturally in their work and sharing photos with the children and families. With supervision, twos may enjoy taking photos as well.

> A **saving shelf or area** as a safe space for children to place projects they may wish to return to or that allows them to view their work over time.

> A **quiet space** where children can decompress, calm down, or relax. It can also be offered if a child is not yet ready to talk through a conflict resolution. This area is typically available for only one child at a time. It is a great space for books, plush toys, and photos of families.

Summary

Facilitating the social and emotional learning and development of very young children, beginning with young infants, is considered by many in the early childhood profession to be one of the most important things teachers do. This chapter focused on the key aspects of this learning and development: the emergence of a sense of self, an understanding of others, and how this happens within a social context. In other words, it is not just about the individual child but the child *with* and *alongside* others. Therefore, the play materials in this chapter included both toys and other resources, most especially *human* resources, such as teachers, peers, and family members that surround each child as they grow.

Suggested Play Materials

Visual Arts

- Beads to string
- Blocks of various shapes, sizes, and types
- Cardboard boxes, tubes, and pieces and PVC pipe
- Chalkboard, large pieces of chalk, and erasers
- Chunky crayons and big nonpermanent markers
- Clay, playdough, slime, and edible putty
- Easels
- Fabric pieces in different textures (e.g., corduroy, satin, denim, faux fur)
- Finger paint, tempera paints, and large, chubby brushes
- Glue, paste, scissors, and tape
- Jumbo craft sticks
- Loose parts
- Natural things (e.g., leaves, pine cones)
- Nuts and bolts (large plastic pieces)
- Paper
- Sensory materials in a variety of patterns, colors, shapes, and textures

Music and Movement

- Instruments to make live music (e.g., guitar, piano, autoharp, recorder)
- Music makers (e.g., wrist or ankle shakers, bells, cymbals, drums)
- Recorded music that reflects children's families, cultures, and communities (e.g., classical, country, gospel, hip-hop, jazz, pop, rock)
- Scarves, streamers, and other things to wave around

Drama

- Dramatic play props (e.g., things to use in the home living area, baby dolls)
- Dress-up clothes and accessories
- Felt boards and stiffened felt figures
- Molded plastic animals
- Puppets and plush animals
- Scarves and colorful fabrics

CHAPTER 9

Play Materials That Encourage Me to Express Myself Creatively

A child sings before it speaks, dances almost before it walks. Music is in our hearts from the beginning.

—Pamela Brown, *The Swish of the Curtain*

From the very young child's perspective, social and emotional learning and development can be summed up as follows: I learn who I am and how I feel. It is a process that begins the moment a child is born and continues throughout their lifetime. According to the Early Childhood Art Educators Issues Group (n.d.), the creative arts "empower children to communicate, represent, and express their thoughts, feelings, and perceptions." These skills, and creative expression in general, are important for emotional intelligence (Geher, Betancourt, & Jewell 2017; Menzer 2015). Emotional intelligence impacts several aspects of children's social and emotional learning and development, including self-awareness, emotional control, motivation, the ability to self-soothe, empathy, and the ability to communicate with and relate to other people (Tominey et al. 2017).

Supporting Creative Expression

- Provide frequent and consistently high-quality creative arts experiences
- Support children in learning to respect and care for tools and materials
- Encourage individual expression
- Talk about the beauty children can see every day in the world around them
- Integrate creative arts throughout the daily routine
- Strive to be more creative yourself in order to model enthusiasm and confidence
- Create a sense of order and beauty in the environment by keeping it uncluttered; displaying beautiful books, posters, and images; and having live plants

This chapter focuses on how you can facilitate multiple aspects of social and emotional learning and development when very young children engage in creative arts activities. Specifically, we discuss play materials that support visual arts (e.g., painting, drawing, building with blocks and other materials, making designs and constructions with clay and sand), music and movement (e.g., listening to and playing musical instruments, dancing and moving to music), and drama (e.g., conversations with exaggerated gestures and emotional expression, imaginative play, storytelling, and puppetry). The materials, ideas, and suggestions in this chapter support children's expanding sense of self as unique individuals through creative expression. Although discussed separately in this chapter, the creative life of the very young child impacts them in a truly holistic way—mind (cognitive), body (physical), as well as spirit and soul (social and emotional).

Young Infants (Security Seekers)

Young infants tend to relax and feel calmed by the voices of their teachers. They love to engage in deep conversations as they coo and babble to their teachers, and young infants enjoy hearing teachers' voices as they listen to stories. They delight in songs being sung to them or music being played as they are rocked and held. Young infants are particularly good at distinguishing sounds, understanding music as different from noise, and recognizing new voices, music, and songs from familiar ones. This ability is strongest during the first six months of life (Kuhl 2011).

Blocks and Sensory Materials

Although young infants have a limited ability to express themselves on their own through visual arts, offer materials with different patterns, colors, shapes, and textures, as recommended in Chapter 5. Block building, considered a form of creative expression, begins when young infants become familiar with the shapes and properties of blocks. Give young infants soft, lightweight, squeezable blocks to build with (Hirsch 1996).

Recorded and Live Music

When using recorded music, whether in the background or as the central focus of an activity, it should be music that reflects diverse languages and cultures. In other words, do not restrict your choices to music specifically made for children. Choose music from multiple genres, especially those enjoyed by the families of the children in your program and the surrounding community (NAEYC 2019a, 2020). There are two primary reasons this is important. First, young children feel a sense of belonging and acceptance when they hear the music their families value (Price & Steed 2016). Second, it exposes them to a diversity of musical styles, sounds, beats, and rhythms.

Play music that supports the current mood and emotional atmosphere in the setting or that purposefully creates a change, like soothing music to calm everyone down or something with a raucous beat to help make everyone more alert. Young infants enjoy passively listening to music, but many also delight in becoming participants in musical experiences with you. When you hold them and move to the music, gently bounce them on a knee so that they experience more fully the beat of the music or tap out a rhythm on the palms of their hands or bottoms of their feet. Young infants don't just *hear* music, they *feel* it as well (Feierabend 2019).

Be sure to play lullabies for young infants. Whether sung to them by you or played softly from a recording, most young infants find lullabies calming and comforting.

> As soon as a lullaby begins, a soothing sense of order infuses the infantile consciousness. The swaying rhythm is close to its own heartbeat, and the quiet melodious sounds [are] a blessed relief from the world's usual racket; the simple, repeating melody is also a source of comfort. (Hewett 2013)

Lullabies help transition young infants to sleep as you pat or rub their bodies while they lie in the crib or as you hold them in your arms and gently sway to the music. According to Lerner and Parlakian (2016), these practices promote attachment between young infants and adults and can occur when you sing lullabies as well as other songs.

Books, Stories, and Conversations

You help young infants begin to appreciate and understand dramatic expression by having interesting conversations with them, telling them stories, and sharing books while holding them on your lap. One of the key definitions of *drama* is that it is "an exciting, emotional, or unexpected series of events or set of circumstances" (Lexico, n.d.). The essence of drama is to stimulate the mind and the imagination. When you hold conversations, tell stories, or read with young infants, use big, exaggerated facial expressions and gestures to make it more dramatic and ignite their curiosity and continued interest (Raising Children Network 2019).

Mobile Infants (Discovery Seekers)

The creative arts are not about following rules, predictability, or control—the skills of academics and schooling (Eisner 2002). With infants, the arts are instead all about exploration and discovery (Feliu-Torruella, Fernández-Santín, & Atenas 2021). Mobile infants, who are all about discovery, are at a perfect age to begin the exploration of art materials and the joy of self-expression.

Process Art Materials

Mobile infants begin their explorations in creative expression with no particular outcome in mind. No product is planned and what emerges is largely irrelevant to them—it is all about the doing. Mobile infants are constructing knowledge and understanding through sensorimotor play involving all of the senses. By working with various art materials (e.g., clay, finger paint, chalk, textured fabrics), the child is coming to appreciate the nature of these things, learning what they do and how to work with them in ways that are fun and interesting. For the most part, mobile infants use only their bodies, in particular their hands, for visual arts expression.

In addition to finger painting and working with clay, mobile infants enjoy crumpling, crinkling, shredding, and tearing regular paper or colorful construction paper. They also like to glue or paste torn bits of paper and other materials like fabric pieces, loose parts, and things from nature (e.g., leaves, twigs, pine cones) to large sheets of art paper to create collages. They love discovering the sticky nature of glue and paste and will spend long minutes with a piece of tape, discovering the sticky side and the nonsticky side! These open-ended sensory experiences with art materials are enjoyable in the moment, and they also prepare the child for years of appreciating and creating their own art.

Music for Movement

Mobile infants are becoming very good at feeling the beat and moving to music. There are few things that capture your attention and delight like when you catch mobile infants swaying and bopping to music! These are times for you to join in with enthusiasm, even if you are across the room. Make eye contact and give a lot of positive verbal encouragement ("Oh, you really like that music, don't you? Look at you dance!") while moving and dancing to the music yourself. Such moments are fun for all involved, and they help mobile infants in the highly significant social and emotional development of *theory of mind*, in which they begin to understand that others have emotions and that these emotions can be shared (Suddendorf & Fletcher-Flinn 2011).

Puppets and Plush Animals

Puppets, plush animals, and molded plastic animals are tools that help mobile infants experience and continue building their understanding of dramatic expression. Use these toys in your storytelling and sharing of books, adopting exaggerated gestures and emotional expressions as the animal characters act out scenes. Gently touch the children with a soft toy or puppet, kissing, nuzzling, and patting them to create a multisensory experience (i.e., auditory, visual, and touch senses) that facilitates sensory integration and makes them part of the drama. The shared experience becomes a truly social occasion as more and more children join the fun.

Using different voices for the characters of a book, or speaking through a puppet, stuffed toy, or plastic animal to tell a story, helps mobile infants begin to see dramatic expression as something different and apart from regular conversational forms of communicating. Children begin to see you or the toy taking on a role in what is essentially a play. You become the baby whale as you use a whale puppet when sharing the book *Baby Beluga* (by Raffi, illustrated by Ashley Wolff). As you read *Farmyard Beat* (by Lindsey Craig, illustrated by Marc Brown), mobile infants see that one person—you—can take on many roles as you use different voices and hold up plastic figures of the animals featured in the story. Such experiences stimulate the imagination of mobile infants, and they delight in laughing along with you and their peers.

Toddlers (Autonomy Seekers)

Creative expression meets the need for autonomy when toddlers are allowed to have some control over their choices of materials and how to use them to express their own thoughts and emotions (Fox & Schirrmacher 2014). By doing these activities alongside peers, they begin to enjoy the social aspects of creative expression as well: seeing what others do with the materials, taking pride in showing off their own creations, laughing and dancing along with others to music, and sharing joy with their peers in early pretend play. Through these activities, toddlers represent ideas and communicate emotions that they typically cannot yet express well verbally (Rymanowicz 2015).

Scaffolded Art Materials

Although toddlers should be allowed to engage in open-ended, process-oriented art to support their need for autonomy, this does not mean that you have no role in helping them express themselves creatively. Toddlers can benefit from simple teacher-guided or teacher-inspired art experiences. From Reggio Emilia educators and their *atelieristas* (art educators), the early childhood field has learned that helping children learn how best to use certain tools and guiding them in different ways to work with materials (i.e., scaffolding) can help them move on to engage in more complex ways of expressing themselves (Vecchi 2010). By scaffolding a child who is struggling or bored and may otherwise quickly move on to something else, you open a door that may encourage them to keep experimenting ("That is a beautiful color, Makayla. Have you tried holding the brush like this? Yes, see how much easier it is to use?" and "Juan and Zuri, look at the caterpillar I made with the playdough! Yes, I just roll it like this, back and forth with this part of my hand").

Art for Young Children

Process-Oriented Art	Product-Oriented Art
■ There's no sample or pattern for the child to follow	■ The child follows a sample or pattern and has instructions
■ Adults don't know what the child will create	■ Adults know what the final product will look like
■ There's no right or wrong way to make the art	■ There's a right way and a wrong way to make the art
■ The art is original every time	■ Adults feel the need to "fix" the art
■ The child explores a variety of interesting materials	

Adapted from Bongiorno (n.d.)

Music with a Beat

Toddlers love to dance and march with their peers in response to music. This is a truly social activity that usually stirs wonderfully positive emotions like laughing and giggling, promoting bonds of friendship and community. Select music that has a strong and easy-to-follow beat. We all know such music—the type that you just cannot help but respond to by tapping your foot or bopping your head. Music with a strong beat, rhythm, and tempo is not just fun, it also supports important fundamental learning related to mathematics and reasoning, including sequencing, counting, and one-to-one correspondence, among other important abilities (Geist, Geist, & Kuznik 2012).

Another fun way for toddlers to follow the beat of the music is with simple musical instruments. There are many instruments for toddlers to use when marching or dancing in a group music experience, including wrist or ankle shakers, bells, cymbals, egg shakers, and maracas. Other instruments are more suitable when toddlers are sitting down, such as small drums, rhythm sticks, xylophones, and chimes. Whether up on their feet or sitting down, toddlers enjoy waving things like colorful streamers or scarves, moving them up, down, side to side, and around in circles. In all cases, emphasize the beat of the music, keeping a strong rhythm for the toddlers to hear and feel.

Stories to Launch Dramas

Vivian Gussin Paley, author and child play advocate, famously brought storytelling together with story acting in her kindergarten (Cooper 2009). The skills to do this can begin as early as toddlerhood. You can use toddlers' emerging understanding of pretend and imaginative play to launch them into the world of creating their own dramas from favorite stories. By this time, children who were read to consistently from early infancy on have developed a love for books, and may have favorite books, authors, and even sometimes poems. Take advantage of toddlers' fascination with stories by encouraging pairs or small groups to take on simple roles to act out or retell the story. Because toddlers are still pre-symbolic in their play, you have a role as "director," helping them sort out parts to play and how to engage in their first dramatizations. You can also utilize felt boards with stiffened felt figures that represent favorite story characters to encourage group participatory storytelling.

By expressing themselves creatively, identity-seeking 2-year-olds come to know themselves more deeply (Kile 2018). Thoughts and emotions about who they are in the context of others, how they feel about themselves, and what they can do emerge in the creative process. Furthermore, the acts involved in creating and sharing their work with others in a safe and noncritical environment allows self-esteem to flourish (Fox & Schirrmacher 2014). They feel, "Wow, I did this! I did this beautiful thing that other people like!"

Blocks and Other Building Materials

Blocks are an essential play and learning material for very young children and an important means for encouraging and supporting creative expression as it relates to social and emotional learning and development. Two-year-olds become increasingly proficient in working with blocks as their spatial reasoning and physical dexterity continue to develop. Using blocks of various types, twos can express themselves creatively in three dimensions. Importantly, block play encourages social interactions among peers, helping them take some of their first steps into engaging cooperatively with others as they construct structures together. At the same time, with your guidance, they begin to practice how to respond appropriately to the mistaken behaviors of others (e.g., invasions of their space, unapproved borrowing of "their" blocks, having their building knocked down by someone) through negotiation, compromise, and forgiveness.

Unit blocks and a variety of other types of blocks and building construction toys (e.g., cardboard bricks, bristle blocks, small plastic blocks that snap together, plastic nuts and bolts) are suitable for 2-year-olds. Other building materials should also be available as play choices for twos at all times. We suggest any number of safe loose parts that can be used in either three-dimensional structures, collages, or other visual art expression. Two-year-olds enjoy documenting their block constructions or other projects—another means of creative expression—through drawing, painting, taking photos, and dictating their thoughts for you to write down. They also enjoy "writing" their own descriptions or stories on paper using chubby crayons or markers.

Mood Music

Twos enjoy listening to music as they draw, paint, and play with clay (Kile 2018). Unlike music that you might select for movement activities (e.g., with a strong rhythm, an easy-to-follow beat), to create the type of mood that inspires the very young artist, softly play background music that is calm and does not have distracting lyrics. Good choices for this are classical music, instrumentals, and sounds from nature (e.g., birdsongs, trickling streams, ocean waves, rainforest sounds).

Music is an effective tool for promoting 2-year-olds' social and cultural identities. Along with other aspects of supporting a diversity-focused curriculum (NAEYC 2019b), remember to share music from a variety of cultures. This includes playing music that twos might hear at home as well as music representative of a variety of cultures and ethnicities (e.g., Asian instrumental music, Brazilian dance music, Hungarian folk music, Native American chanting), whether represented in the setting or not. You may wish to invite family members or people from the community to play instruments, sing, or dance. Two-year-olds take special pride in having the music that represents their own family, language, and culture performed live and in person in their child care environment.

Props to Support Dramatic Play

The emergence of symbolic thought after the age of 2 allows for the rapid development of increasingly sophisticated dramatic play. Twos know how to make stories come alive. As Magda Gerber (n.d.) suggested, "Let the child be the scriptwriter, the director, and the actor in his own play." Their imaginations can be sparked by having plenty of dress-up clothes and accessories (e.g., hats, purses, ties, shoes) and dramatic play props (e.g., play food and kitchen equipment, baby dolls, a doctor's kit). Increasingly, 2-year-olds begin to take on specific roles in their cooperative play with peers, both giving and assigning parts to play ("*I* mommy! *You* baby!" "Nooo! *I* mommy!"). As with block play, these early forays into cooperative play with peers can be fraught with plenty of high drama in terms of emotional outbursts and hurt feelings. You will need to supervise carefully as 2-year-olds work to become more skilled at cooperative play.

Summary

Creative expression enhances the quality of life from our first moments on earth, hearing the gentle voice of a loved one as they sing a lullaby, feeling the rock and sway of our bodies in the arms of a beloved family member as they keep time to the beat of the music playing in the background, and sensing the comfort and security that comes from a well-ordered, predictable routine. From these earliest moments, the child should be surrounded by and encouraged to engage in creative expression in a number of ways, particularly through the visual arts, music and movement, and drama. Creative expression facilitates social skill development (e.g., cooperation, positive interaction with others), supports emotional development (e.g., appreciation for beauty and order in the surrounding world, feelings of connectedness to community and culture, emotional regulation), promotes the ability to take multiple perspectives and an openness to new ideas and people, and builds self-esteem and self-confidence that can last a lifetime (Fox & Schirrmacher 2014; Menzer 2015).

Suggested Play Materials

- Aquarium or terrarium for animals like fish and crabs

- Bird feeders, wind chimes, and light prisms

- Gathering baskets for collecting, sorting, and carrying

- Indoor plants

- Insect carriers and bug viewers

- Live animals (e.g., bunnies, guinea pigs)

- Molded plastic animals (e.g., birds, bugs, dinosaurs)

- Natural settings nearby to visit for walks and field trips (e.g., beaches, farms, forests, gardens, neighborhood parks, playgrounds, ponds)

- Outdoor garden for planting, watering, weeding, and harvesting

- Photographs, posters, and books depicting the natural world

- Playsets of outdoor scenes (e.g., camping, farm)

- Sandbox for digging, filling, and sifting

- Science area with items from nature

- Science tools (e.g., binoculars, funnels, magnifying glasses, measuring cups and spoons, squeezable bottles, tongs)

- Sensory table

- Stuffed animals and animal puppets

CHAPTER 10

Play Materials That Connect Me to Nature and Science

Time in nature is not leisure time; it's an essential investment in our children's health (and also, by the way, in our own).

—Richard Louv, *Last Child in the Woods: Saving Our Children from Nature-Deficit Disorder*

Exploring and being in nature is invaluable, not only because it is a gateway to learning about things like biology, geology, or ecology, but because it opens doors to our understanding of ourselves and our place within the world. Forming a positive relationship with the natural world and living things early in life impacts lifetime notions of who we are as social beings, how we see ourselves in relation to others, and what it means to care for and be compassionate about others and the world around us (Thompson & Thompson 2007). Appreciating nature and feeling joyful and content when in nature sustains our emotional well-being and is at the very heart and soul of defining who we are and who we become as human beings (Louv 2008; Rivkin 2014).

This chapter presents play materials and ways to use them to help very young children develop a positive relationship with and an understanding and appreciation of nature and the natural world. We emphasize play materials that will support budding notions of stewardship (i.e., taking care of all living things) through the development of habits and behaviors that protect the natural environment.

Young infants first experience nature and the wider world around them while in the arms of the caring adults in their lives. When introducing young infants to nature and the natural world, look for their communication cues, such as signs that a child is relaxed, frightened, or becoming overstimulated. The goal is to help young infants develop a positive relationship with and appreciation for nature, so do your best to help them have positive experiences with the natural world.

Be careful not to pass on your own fears and biases about nature and its animals. Young infants are very much at one with their environment, and they are gradually developing awareness that they are separate and apart from other people and other things. Thus, young infants are highly in tune with the emotions of their teachers and take their cues about how to feel and respond from them. When sharing encounters with nature and the natural world, young infants will sense, for instance, your positive feelings of joy and amazement, just as they will your more negative reactions, such as fear or disgust.

Stay Calm

For security-seeking young infants who are highly attuned to their teacher's emotions and reactions, it is important to stay calm even when encountering something in the natural world that may truly be dangerous or a real cause for concern (e.g., an approaching storm, a poisonous snake along the pathway, a skunk wandering into the play yard). Adopting a neutral, matter-of-fact tone even when encounters with nature might be dangerous helps young infants feel safer and more secure.

Outdoor Play Experiences

The best place for young infants to experience the natural world is to be in it—outdoors! All children, even young infants, must have time outdoors, whether that time is spent in an outdoor play yard, on a patio or deck, or during a buggy or stroller walk. As long as they are dressed appropriately for the weather and sunscreen covers all exposed skin, children benefit from being outdoors. They begin to form their first conceptions of nature from feeling the sun and breeze on their skin, seeing puffy clouds swirling overhead, smelling newly cut grass and flowers blooming, and hearing the sounds of birds chirping nearby. They will delight in exploring blades of grass and dandelions, the texture of the dirt or sand, or the crunchiness of fallen leaves around them.

You can facilitate young infants' social and emotional learning and development when outdoors through shared experiences, primarily through conversation. Consider the following example of a teacher enjoying a buggy ride experience with young infants:

"The sun feels so warm! Doesn't it, friends?" Mr. Iroh says to a small group of infants during their daily walk. "I love the gentle breeze; it will keep us from getting too hot. Do you feel it on your skin? Oh, Jade, I see the breeze is blowing your hat. Let me tie it to your chin so it doesn't blow away."

A little farther down the path, he continues, "Did you hear something, Luis? Let's all listen. What is it? Oh, I see; I think it's a bunch of birds making all that noise. Do you all hear that? It sounds a bit like . . ." Mr. Iroh imitates a squawking noise, and the children babble and coo in response. "You think that's funny?" He squawks again. "Oh my! Just look at the birds, they're all taking off and flying away together, way up high in the sky!" he says while raising his hands up in the air. "I wonder why. Where are they going?"

"What are you looking at, Seraphina? What do you see?" he asks. "Oh look, everyone. Seraphina spotted two squirrels racing each other up that big tree where the birds were!" Mr. Iroh draws the children's attention toward the tree. "Around and around they go! I wonder, do you think it was the squirrels that scared the birds and made them fly away?"

Although this teacher is the only one speaking in this example, it is not simple chatter—it is a back-and-forth conversation. He knows the children well and responds to cues from individual children. By paying careful attention to facial expressions, body language, and the early vocalizations of the young infants, the teacher observes what drew the interest of individual children and comments upon those specific things. The teacher speaks to the children in a natural tone as he names objects, provides context, uses vivid descriptors, and models observation skills and curiosity. He shares his positive feelings of wonder and joy in their communal encounter with nature.

Remember also the value of silence and to sometimes let nature speak for itself. Quiet moments outdoors are just as important to a young infant's development of a positive relationship with the natural world as conversations. It is in moments of quiet, of stillness, that children have the opportunity to learn to listen with their hearts and experience the sense of contentment that can be felt from just being in nature.

Mobile Infants (Discovery Seekers)

Because mobile infants discover new things using all of their senses, direct encounters with nature and natural items need to be carefully planned and supervised. Now that they can move about fairly freely, it is important for you to be extra cautious about safety while providing access to interesting discoveries in their environment. With the increasing ability to participate in joint or shared attention with you or a peer comes an important social development: drawing attention to what they want another person to look at by pointing at it or using some other, primarily nonverbal means. Mobile infants can now engage socially in an experience or activity in a way they could not before.

Inside Materials

Include toys representing the natural world of the mobile infant's environment, such as plush or molded plastic miniature replicas of animals, bugs, birds, dinosaurs, and sea creatures. You can place these items on shelves and fill baskets, tubs, or other containers with them. Board books displayed on the bookshelves should include nonfiction books about plant and animal life, habitats, and various natural environments, as well as stories of diverse young children enjoying nature. Display photographs and posters that realistically depict living creatures and nature, not highly stylized, symbolic, or cartoonish images. The selection of books, posters, and other images should include local flora and fauna that the children are most likely to see in the environments where they live.

Two other important components of the environment for the discovery-seeking mobile infant are the science area and sensory table (or tub). These can be used to expose children to a variety of objects from nature and encourage social interactions among pairs and small groups of children. Suggested items for the science area for mobile infants include bones, seashells, rocks, leaves, flowers, logs and branches, seedpods, pine cones, and gourds and other squash. Things that you find that the children love and never tire of exploring should remain permanent fixtures in the science area. A fish aquarium is an example of this, as are large bar magnets and tools such as magnifying glasses. Other objects should be changed out frequently to attract new interest and new opportunities for discovery.

Infants and Toddlers at Play

Fill your sensory table with a variety of natural materials so children can discover different textures and smells, including sand, water, leaves, mulch, flowers, grass, soil, mud, and (in some climates) snow. Because everything still makes it into their mouths at this age, be extra careful that all items are clean and bug and pesticide free and that they do not constitute a choking hazard.

Window on Nature

Discoveries about the natural world can be made through the setting's windows. An added enjoyment is sharing this experience with others—teachers and friends—made possible because of mobile infants' increased ability for shared attention. So much can happen right outside the windows in your setting: birds fly by; the weather changes; someone walks by with a dog on a leash; a bunny hops through the yard; a worker cuts the grass, tends the garden, or shovels snow. You can also put things outside the window to attract children's attention, like bird feeders, wind chimes, and prisms that refract sunlight. Such materials provide endless potential for discovering nature and the natural world.

All of these things also offer opportunities to hold pleasant conversations with discovery-seeking mobile infants, conversations that can be revisited and retold over and over ("Let's tell your mommy about that big yellow bumblebee you saw today!" or "Do you remember how noisy it was when the rain hit the window?").

Toddlers (Autonomy Seekers)

When setting up experiences with nature for toddlers, keep in mind both their need for autonomy ("*Me* do it!") and the safety concerns that come with their desire for independence. Toddlers are highly capable young investigators:

> If you [. . .] take a random 15-month-old, just sit and watch them for 10 minutes and count out how many experiments, how much thinking you see going on, and it will put the most brilliant scientist to shame. (Gopnik 2013)

Although toddlers have short attention spans (an average of three to five minutes), their ability to focus on one thing is increasing. This allows you more opportunities to use scaffolding and modeling to build connections to nature.

Science Tools

Toddlers are moving beyond simple discovery learning to experimentation and are ready and eager to use some of the tools of science to learn more about the natural world. In the science area for toddlers, you can include child-size and sturdy versions of things like magnifying glasses, funnels, tongs, eyedroppers, squeezable bottles, measuring spoons and cups, large bar magnets, and insect carriers and bug viewers.

Water play is particularly useful in promoting both individual experimentation and learning socially through shared experiences. Toddlers begin to understand the nature and power of water from playing with it and through experimentation using a variety of tools (e.g., things to pour from and into, PVC pipes, waterwheels, things that float and sink). A water source for this playful experimentation can be natural, like a pond or puddle, or set up in a small tub, children's pool, or sensory table.

Socially oriented parallel play begins to spontaneously occur when you set up experiences around natural science explorations and pairs or small groups gather and enjoy the activities together. As toddlers play alongside one another through such encounters, they begin to imitate what others are doing, building idea upon idea, skill upon skill. They are not only modeling for one another, but peers and the materials themselves are scaffolding the learning of each individual toddler.

Ideas to scaffold young children's learning include

> Suggesting an idea (e.g., "I wonder what happens if you turn that pipe the other way. Yes, like that. Wow, did you see that? The water runs faster, doesn't it!")

> Asking an open-ended question (e.g., "What do you think is happening? Why isn't the water coming through the pipe? Oh, yes, that was it, you found the problem! It was plugged up!")

> Providing a tool that may help them be successful in accomplishing whatever they are trying to do (e.g., "Here, friends, you may want to try these scoopers. I think they may help you get the water in the pitcher.")

Containers are another excellent science tool. As noted before, toddlers love to gather and collect objects and then carry them from place to place (Karasik et al. 2012; Zorn 2012). This can be particularly fun when you are on a nature walk around the neighborhood or just in the play yard. It is important to provide plenty of gathering baskets, bags, and containers for this. Toddlers can be encouraged to collect natural items that you and the children together can sort and display on the science table. A child will feel proud knowing they are the one that found a particular object, as well as a sense of contribution from placing it among items collected by friends.

Living Things

If you are able to bring living creatures and plants into your setting, you are giving toddlers a gift that will last a lifetime. This is particularly true if the very young child has little or no exposure to animals at home or in their community. Purewal and colleagues (2017) found that having a relationship with animals contributes to cognitive and social and emotional development, especially self-esteem, social competence, and more positive social interaction and social play.

Bringing Animals into the Program Setting

Animals That Are Appropriate Pets for Children from Birth to Age 3

- Bearded dragons
- Domesticated rats
- Fish (especially bettas, danios, goldfish, guppies, and tetras)
- Guinea pigs
- Hermit crabs
- Rabbits

Animals That Should Be Avoided with Children from Birth to Age 3

- Animals that may spread bacteria, parasites, or viruses, such as most amphibians, birds, chickens, ducks, ferrets, and reptiles
- Animals that are venomous or toxin producing, such as certain frogs, lizards, snakes, and spiders
- Animals that are stray, aggressive, wild, or unpredictable, such as bats, coyotes, feral cats, foxes, and racoons
- Nonhuman primates, such as monkeys and apes

Adapted from CDC (2020) and Remitz (2013)

In addition to the safety of the children, including their allergies, please consider the safety of any living creatures in your setting. Remember that toddlers are working hard at practicing many physical skills and may be clumsy at times. It is important to balance toddlers' need for independence with careful supervision. You will need to be very direct in your instructions with toddlers as you teach and model for them how best to treat a live animal and the specifics of how to care for them (e.g., "Sit right here, please, and put your hands out like this. Now, you can hold the bunny. Gentle now, don't squeeze too tight, just pat. Yes, that's right," or "Use just a pinch of food in the fish bowl. Yes, like that. They don't eat much!").

Safety Tips for Interacting with Animals

- Before bringing any animal into your program, consider any allergies or illnesses children may have and speak with their families as needed for precautionary measures.
- Anyone who has touched an animal or their habitat should immediately wash their hands. Help or supervise young children with this task to make sure it is done thoroughly.
- Never wash animal supplies or habitats in the same sink where food is prepared.
- Clean and disinfect any area an animal has been in contact with.
- Always carefully supervise children who are holding or petting animals.
- Make sure all animals have regular veterinary checkups.

Adapted from CDC (2020)

Twos (Identity Seekers)

Two-year-olds are becoming increasingly social, developing special friendships with particular peers. They love to engage in pretend play, mostly acting out things modeled for them by adults and older children in their lives. Scaffolding and modeling are very important modes of learning for twos, but just as with mobile infants, there is also a need for you to provide more direct instruction at times.

Things to Care for and About

Under adult supervision, 2-year-olds are able to take on a greater role and most can be trusted with some responsibility in the daily care of plants and animals. With you looking on and reminding them as needed what to do, they can feed pets, water indoor plants, and help tend to the outdoor garden. This type of activity allows them to take on the role of a caretaker, adding this to their growing sense of who they are. This notion of being the caretaker of other living things will be internalized as part of the child's social and emotional identity, and it is an important life lesson that cannot begin too early.

In addition to developing an identity as a caretaker for animals and plants, twos are at a very good age to start learning to care for and about the environment more broadly. Although they are certainly not ready for lectures on saving the rainforest or the polar ice caps, they are capable of early moral and ethical thinking, particularly in terms of having a sense of what is right and wrong (Warneken & Tomasello 2008). Twos are also capable of empathy and engage in numerous prosocial behaviors (McMullen et al. 2009). You can build on these characteristics and help twos become socially conscious about the environment and all the people and living things within it.

This awareness begins primarily with you modeling behaviors, such as finding creative ways to reuse or repurpose old materials, picking up trash you find on the playground, and turning off lights and the water tap when not in use. Although you may do these things out of habit, as often as possible, describe what you are doing and why you are doing it; for instance, "Let's turn the water off while we soap up our hands. We shouldn't let it run when we don't need it," or "You can use the back of these papers I got from the office. We need to save paper because we use it for so many projects." You can also very directly help twos get in the habit of sorting and recycling certain things like paper and plastic, putting them into appropriate containers that are separate from trash.

Walks and Field Trips

Splashing through a puddle, squishing bare feet in the mud, stomping on ice to crack it, digging toes in the sand, rolling in the grass, or crunching through dry leaves are all wonderful ways for twos to learn about and enjoy themselves in the natural world. Sometimes these experiences just happen naturally out in the play yard. Other times, consider expanding the contexts and types of nature your children experience by taking twos on a nature walk or field trip. There is just so much to see and share with others on a visit to city parks, local playgrounds, farms, orchards, beaches, botanical gardens, or the woods. Twos cannot help but find things that amaze them and stretch their understanding of nature and sense the joy that can be found in sharing these marvels with others.

Most twos will now participate fully in conversations with you, both verbally and nonverbally. Even twos with limited speech are usually able to be understood by you and their friends about the enjoyment they experience on a walk or field trip. Twos will often want you to write down what they say about what they see. Later, they may attempt to draw it, and they are usually very excited to revisit and talk about the experience afterward with you and their friends. This modeling of recording observations and engaging in reflective discussions about those observations is important in building the inquiry skills in science.

Gardening

Whether you have a plot of earth suitable for planting, a raised bed, or pots you can place on a sunny windowsill or roof of your building, twos will love being gardeners. Twos can participate fully in digging holes for planting seeds and seedlings, watering plants, weeding, and harvesting vegetables, fruit, herbs, or flowers. Although twos are ready to engage in these tasks *mostly* independently, you should still be nearby to make sure they do not, for instance, overwater plants, tromp all over young sprouts, or pick produce or flowers that are not quite ready to be picked. After harvesting produce from the garden, twos can help clean and ready it for eating or give it to you or the program's cook to prepare for a healthy snack or meal to be shared by all (Baker & Futterman 2013). They will enjoy arranging flowers they have picked for the lunchtime table or preparing bouquets to bring home to their families or give to important visitors.

Twos benefit in many ways from gardening. They learn so much about the natural world: how things grow, how our food comes from the earth, and that plants are living things that must be cared for. They also come to understand that gardening is a shared, social activity done by a group of people working together in community. Having and working toward common goals is important social learning for twos. Emotionally, many twos will come to find tending a garden calming and richly rewarding, contributing to personal enjoyment and boosting their self-confidence by eliciting a sense of pride and accomplishment.

How Does Your Garden Grow?

Popular Plants for a Children's Garden

Selecting what to have in your garden will depend on your climate and the size of your gardening area. Here are some suggestions you might consider.

Flowers	Fruit Plants	Herbs	Vegetables
Coneflowers	Blueberry	Basil	Carrots
Lamb's ears	Strawberry	Chives	Cucumbers
Marigolds	Tomato	Dill	Green beans
Nasturtiums		Lemon balm	Lettuce
Snapdragons	**Fruit Trees**	Oregano	Potatoes
Petunias	Apple	Parsley	Pumpkins
Strawflowers	Cherry	Rosemary	Snap peas
Sunflowers	Orange	Thyme	Zucchini
	Pear		

Common Plants That Are Dangerous for Children

Azaleas	Dieffenbachia	Mistletoe
Begonias	English ivy	Morning glories
Caladiums	Easter lilies	Oleander
Carnations	Foxgloves	Peace lilies
Daffodils	Geraniums	Philodendron
Dahlias	Holly	Pothos
Daisies	Irises	Rhododendrons

At this age, food preferences and eating habits that can last a lifetime are being established. Young twos who garden also tend to want to taste the foods they grow, encouraging some who may otherwise be picky eaters to try new things (Robinson-O'Brien, Story, & Heim 2009). They are more likely to love the things they have worked so hard and waited so patiently to grow! Advocates addressing childhood obesity promote gardening with young children, including toddlers and twos, as a way to help them develop healthy habits around food and have fun getting exercise in the sunshine and fresh air.

Summary

Forming a positive relationship with nature and living things is an essential part of very young children's growing understanding of who they are in relation to other people and living things. It also awakens them to the ideas of care and compassion about the world around them, as well as their place and responsibility within it.

In Your Words

Kim Anderson, teacher, and Abby Jenney, program coordinator, of the SUNY Cortland Child Care Center in Cortland, New York, reflect on supporting social and emotional development in infant and toddler settings.

Social and emotional development is a broad spectrum that encompasses sharing and turn-taking, creating positive relationships, working toward empathy, conversing and storytelling, problem solving, and learning about our emotions and what to do with them. Our center's learning environment is set up in a way that allows both individual and group play and discovery.

As teachers, making ourselves open and available all day as facilitators and a support system for children guarantees the best outcomes for each child to develop and understand themselves as individuals. Social and emotional skills are the basic building blocks that help each person succeed in the world. When a child is able to successfully identify and manage their emotions, carry on conversations with others, and empathize with those around them, they can truly find their place in the world and be happy.

Toddlers do everything in a big way. In our toddler room, teachers respond appropriately to the emotions toddlers experience throughout their day, even the tough ones. We facilitate interactions among peers, for instance, by sitting close as children build in the block area or play with materials in the sensory table. However, we do not always intervene in every moment. When a situation arises, we assess how the children are responding to each other. We stay near children as they play so they know that they have support when needed, while at the same time communicating that they have the courage and skills to solve their problems independently.

In our room for 2-year-olds, we often see a wide range of emotions as children's language is growing rapidly and they are learning more self-control over their emotions and reactions. It is our job to help guide them through the process with different activities, toys, visual cues, and resources, as well as to show children it is okay to express a wide variety of emotions.

Books and stories are particularly helpful play resources. We talk with the children about how we think the characters in a story might be feeling and draw attention to feelings with prompts such as "Look at their faces. How do you think they feel?" This helps us to begin to label basic emotions children experience every day and allows children to share their own experiences and emotions. Within our room of mostly 2-year-olds, we introduce social stories that feature children in our setting to help teach them about identifying emotions. These social stories can be specific to one child or generalized to the entire class. We are also using them to help children whose lives are changing. For example, one child will soon have a new baby sister at home. We share a story that acknowledges the changes that are happening, such as mommy's tummy getting bigger, a crib being set up, and how siblings can help. Topics of other social stories include things to do when you are upset, how to calm down, and turn-taking. When teachers introduce these skills to very young children, it helps set them up for future development of social and emotional skills in preschool.

PART FOUR

Physical Learning and Development

Suggested Play Materials

- Baby play gyms or mobiles
- Balance beams
- Balls of all shapes, sizes, and textures
- Blocks (e.g., cardboard, wood)
- Bubbles
- Carpeted bins
- Circle discs for use as stepping-stones, in games, for counting, in obstacle courses, and more
- Lightweight baskets
- Loft with ramp and stairs
- Loose parts (e.g., large wooden spoons, metal bowls, tree blocks)
- Low shelves
- Mirrors
- Musical instruments
- Pulley system with bucket
- Rattles and things that make sounds
- Real tools (e.g., brooms and dustpans, mallets, rakes, shovels, watering cans)
- Scarves
- Sensory materials
- Soft or foam mats
- Swings
- Teething rings
- Tricycles without pedals and seated scooters
- Tunnels
- Yoga flash cards

CHAPTER 11

Play Materials That Help Me Develop My Gross Motor Skills

Enjoy the way infants develop and learn when they are allowed to move at their own time and in their own way.

—Magda Gerber, *Dear Parent: Caring for Infants with Respect*

Gross motor development and learning (whole body movement that involves large muscles) is a fascinating domain because it is so easy to observe growth over time. This chapter showcases the journey of large muscle movement from the earliest stages of life to the child's third year. Beginning in utero, the fetus experiences reflexes and coordinated muscle movements that allow them to engage with the environment of the womb (Robinson & Kleven 2005). After birth, young infants shift their movement patterns, adjusting to the sensations of gravity and friction while adapting to a brand-new environment. Over the next three years, the child will identify what their body is capable of as they acquire new skills and their central nervous system matures (Schmidt & Lee 2011). You have a role in supporting these important changes as movement becomes a central component of how very young children investigate, communicate, and connect to others (Adolph & Robinson 2015). The open-ended play materials discussed in this chapter strengthen children's muscles and posture, motivating and challenging young children as they experience gross motor learning and development.

Gross motor movement begins with involuntary reflexes that prepare the young infant for future voluntary movement. For security-seeking young infants, reflexes revolve around survival, allowing them to signal their needs, put their bodies in safe positions, or attract their teachers' attention (Gerber, Wilks, & Erdie-Lalena 2010). These spontaneous movements are crucial in developing later movement patterns as young infants continue to become increasingly familiar with their environments. Reflexes also aid neural communication between both sides of the brain (Kanemaru, Watanabe, & Taga 2012). Working primarily in the arms of their teacher or with them nearby, young infants need designated safe spaces to move and explore. With this important guideline in mind, we selected materials for young infants that respect what they are capable of doing and allow freedom of movement while in close contact with you.

Soft or Foam Mats

Supporting gross motor exploration with young infants can be a nerve-wracking experience for some. Until quite recently, baby holders or containment devices were popular in infant environments. These included infant chairs, car seats, bouncy baby hammocks, swings, and even special pillows for propping the young infant in specific positions. While designed to keep babies safe, many of the devices that restrain the movement of young infants have been found to be more dangerous than supportive and have also been connected to delays in gross motor development (HHS 2018; Lansbury 2009).

Support young infants' evolving gross motor exploration by putting them on a washable, soft mat on their backs under your direct supervision. Follow the infant's cues for needed support and closeness by lying down or sitting on the floor next to the child. Offer comforting songs and materials, maintaining eye contact as they explore their environment. This allows them to problem solve with their bodies in a space that is comfortable, safe, and inviting. Without

the restriction of straps and devices, the young infant is free to wiggle, shift, and move freely. Under your close supervision, the child can begin to trust their ability to make decisions with their bodies and execute movement at their own pace. Honoring the gross motor needs of young infants provides the blueprint for all future movement.

Rattles and Things That Make Sounds

While shaking a rattle, a young infant begins to discover that certain movements result in certain outcomes, connecting the body and the brain as they learn about perception. Young infants need repeated exposure to experiences and materials that engage their senses and curiosity. To support this development, hold the rattle in a variety of positions, focusing on different parts of the child's body and mobility.

To give a young infant a more tactile experience, place the rattle down by the child's feet when they are kicking and wiggling their toes where they may randomly make contact with it. Alternately, place the rattle on the floor or shake it gently just out of the infant's reach to encourage them to reach for the rattle and explore problem solving.

Holding a rattle over the midline of a young infant ignites core abdominal muscles as they lift their arms to respond. Bringing objects closer to the center of their body promotes focus and control (Bambach et al. 2016). *Crossing the midline* is a phrase used to describe being able to use arms or legs to reach across the middle of the body and cross over to the opposite side. This becomes a crucial skill for young infants as they become more aware of their bodies and continue to work toward gaining a higher level of stability and more complex bilateral (two-sided) movement (Lerner & Parlakian 2016). Crossing the midline while in play benefits every area of development, creating more neural pathways in the brain to store knowledge and build muscle memory.

During these types of engagements, pause frequently to check in with the young infant, observing how their body is responding to the activity. By familiarizing yourself with children's individual cues, you may adjust the position of the child's body if they seem uncomfortable, add or remove stimulating materials, or notice when a child needs a break from gross motor exploration and wants to be held. These adaptations honor the changing needs of the child, prevent overstimulation, extend meaningful engagement, and maintain a sense of connection throughout play.

Mobile Infants (Discovery Seekers)

Mobile infants experience a new level of joy in the freedom they now have as they engage more directly and independently with social situations, spaces, and play materials. Although crawling is most commonly thought of when thinking about this phase of development, keep in mind that mobile infants can move in a variety of ways. Some children prefer to roll from one location to another. Others primarily use arms and upper body muscles to pull themselves forward. You may even witness an infant who prefers to move from sitting to standing, starting to cruise and squat, working toward walking without the process of crawling (Adolph & Robinson 2015). For this age group, we selected materials that are open ended and support the child's pressing need to engage their entire body in play.

Loose Parts

Loose parts encourage mobile infants to explore their world through sensorimotor play in ways that are personally meaningful (Daly & Beloglovsky 2016). Being able to sit independently or with little support at about 7 months old, the mobile infant now has hands free to reach, grab, and bring items closer to their bodies to inspect (Case-Smith 2010). Because distant objects become more accessible, place interesting objects throughout the learning space and encourage mobile infants to actively seek them out. They benefit from both the physical effort required to get the objects and the number of senses that are ignited as they inspect them.

Loose parts have no predetermined way they should be used; instead, they offer "unlimited play possibilities" (Daly & Beloglovsky 2016, 3). Mobile infants continuously seek out these materials, preferring those that adapt and change with their growing needs. Offer loose parts that are safe, avoiding those with detachable parts and small pieces. Large wooden spoons, metal bowls, tree blocks, scarves, clay, fabric, small baskets, carpet squares, and natural materials such as flowers, leaves, and pine cones are all considered loose parts. Each discovery provides a novel experience for the child, targeting their current exploration of physical competency. As Magda Gerber (2003) advised, play materials that are open ended are another way to build trust with the infant by showing that you recognize and respect the child's need to follow their own instincts and explore in ways that feel comfortable for them.

Lofts

As mobile infants continue to work on strengthening their core muscles and sense of balance, lofts offer a new means to explore emerging skills (Gill, Adolph, & Vereijken 2009). Select a loft that is easily taken apart and put together in multiple configurations so you can change it to meet the needs of the children in your setting. Start small, beginning with a basic structure, and then add elements over time, such as stairs or tunnels that appropriately challenge your group of children.

A carpeted ramp can provide any number of intriguing challenges, especially as multiple mobile infants join the play. Adding more bodies on the incline creates quite a puzzle for them to solve. Encourage children to maneuver their bodies around peers and help them adapt their movements to reach a goal (Gill, Adolph, & Vereijken 2009). The walls of the loft can be swapped out to increase visibility or even offer a new climbing experience. Swap panels with wooden bars, mirrored panels, and carpeted panels to offer a variety of exploratory experiences and extend the level of physical engagement.

Placing the loft in different locations in your setting adds a new perspective of your space for the children, such as placing the loft near a window to allow children to look outside. There is no rush to add more features to this play material until the children begin showing a need for more challenges. If there is a mobile infant in the group who is more hesitant to take risks with their body, try placing baskets of intriguing materials at the top of the loft. The possibility of discovering something new may spark their curiosity and ease any reluctance they feel. As safety is a priority, remember to stay close to children as they climb, remaining calm and encouraging as you give young infants space for gentle tumbling, risk-taking, and experimenting.

Considerations for Climbing

- Anchor furniture to the walls to stabilize and secure it, allowing for safer climbing.

- Never place a child onto a climbing feature. Instead, encourage the child to use their own bodies to problem solve how to climb it. If a child cannot climb up on their own, they cannot climb down safely.

- Always stay near children as they climb.

- Coach children to take small, easy steps when they are feeling frustrated; this can help them refocus and persist.

- Soft mats can provide a safe space for children to recognize their physical limits and experience falling, cause and effect, and continuous problem solving. Mats can also prevent injuries in more adventurous children.

- If the way a child is choosing to climb is not safe, find a way to modify this choice in a safe manner. Can you offer it outdoors? Can you add mats or clear the area of hazards? Is there a way to engage the muscles they want to use in a different context?

Toddlers (Autonomy Seekers)

As toddlerhood approaches, children are beginning to build a repertoire of movement methods based solely on hands-on experiences and plenty of trial and error. Movement begins to take a slightly different meaning, however, as toddlers begin to seek out opportunities for themselves to express their autonomy. At times, this can result in some emotional disagreements as you support toddlers in making safe choices and setting appropriate boundaries for their bodies. Beyond keeping children safe, however, it is also your responsibility to provide opportunities for toddlers to do things on their own, freely explore autonomous movement, and feel respected in their need for independence.

Balls of All Shapes and Sizes

As toddlers continue to grow and develop control and strength throughout their bodies, balls become the perfect material to support overall gross motor development. They are also great tools for redirecting children engaged in unsafe or inappropriate throwing exploration (e.g., throwing items like blocks, toys, or food). As a toddler's abilities change and expand, their experimentation with balls may change as well. Keep play child directed and open ended by following the lead of the child and allowing space for the type of exploration they are focusing on. If a toddler is more intrigued with picking up balls and dropping them to the floor, for example, allow this play to happen at their own pace, providing many opportunities to explore this work while adding variety. This may mean introducing different types of balls or changing the environment in which the child can explore with the ball (e.g., indoors, outdoors, up a ramp or hill).

Bringing balls outdoors can provide a brand-new experience for toddlers. As they experiment with exerting more and more energy behind throwing or kicking a ball, they see it roll a greater distance, reach greater heights, or perhaps even disappear out of sight. They hypothesize about what mechanics are necessary for different types of movement (such as throwing a ball harder, softer, lower, or higher) and how throwing a ball outside is different from rolling it inside into the hands of a teacher sitting nearby on the floor. This study of cause and effect brings greater awareness to toddler bodies, while simultaneously strengthening their large muscles (DiCarlo, Stricklin, & Reid 2006).

Allow toddlers ample space to experiment with throwing, bouncing, and rolling without interruption. Place ball bins in areas of the room where this exploration is appropriate and easily accessible for toddlers. Having balls as a safe option for gross motor development will allow you to easily redirect unsafe throwing exploration while providing a supportive environment that honors the changing physical needs of toddlers.

Tricycles Without Pedals and Seated Scooters

As toddlers seek mastery of their ability to balance and shift their weight, they naturally begin to explore materials that add new challenges, allowing them to gain strength and confidence. Seated scooters add variability to movement patterns as they allow for more fluid movement in comparison to what the toddler feels while walking on a flat surface (Adolph & Robinson 2015). Allow open exploration of this material, supporting each child's capabilities and comfort level as they decide how they wish to engage and what they are ready for in terms of using seated scooters or tricycles. You may need to offer a stable hand to a toddler who is independently attempting to climb onto the seat, move obstacles as they experiment with scooting backward, or even create a large open space for toddlers to tip scooters over as they investigate how the wheels move.

As their drive for more intensive gross motor experiences grows, toddlers are drawn toward opportunities that call for problem solving with different areas of their bodies. Children modify their body positions, relocate their centers of gravity, and create a sturdy support system with legs and planted feet. Support toddlers further in this development of body exploration and directionality by staying nearby and creating safe spaces for them to use seated scooters while maintaining an awareness of surrounding peers. If there is not enough room in your indoor environment, take seated scooters outdoors to support toddlers' need to move their lower bodies. This play material provides a whole new experience once toddlers are able to maneuver their bodies with ease, allowing them to feel the thrill of going fast and independently getting to where they want to go.

Twos (Identity Seekers)

For this section of gross motor play, the materials featured continue to support growing muscles as well as the cultivation of self-expression. Twos are transitioning from exploring how they can move to exploring how they as individuals specifically wish to move.

Real Tools

Toy tools made for young children typically lack the ability to accomplish much of anything beyond being a prop for pretend play. Two-year-olds enjoy experimenting with real tools—those they have seen adults use—to perform tasks as they continue to look for projects that are personally meaningful. They are fascinated with the tools adults use and are naturally drawn toward any opportunity to engage with these tools through hands-on exploration and experimentation.

Closely supervise twos' open exploration using tools, such as real (but child-size) metal shovels and rakes, mallets, kitchen utensils, and even power tools with the appropriate structured context and supervision (Schaefer 2016). Support 2-year-olds in their growing ability to control their arms and hands by offering safety gear while they work. Child-size work gloves, safety goggles, and aprons not only keep the child physically safe, they also provide a reminder to practice taking responsibility for their own body as they work.

These tools and many others can facilitate children's gross motor movement by adding precision and precaution to their skill sets to prevent injury. They learn to have respect for the objects as well as for what they are capable of doing with them. Real tools provide experiences that encourage the continued practice of object control, activating muscles used in lifting, carrying, pushing, pulling, and transporting objects (Haywood & Getchell 2014). Providing tools that allow 2-year-olds to stretch their physical capabilities will assist them in adapting and assessing what their bodies can do in the moment to accomplish their goals.

Yoga Flash Cards

As 2-year-olds seek to express themselves as individuals, offer a variety of gross motor exploration opportunities that embrace creativity in motion. Yoga cards offer a novel experience and support emerging skills of modeling and observing. When introducing yoga cards, first describe the image on the card. Then, explain what areas of the body the children need to move and describe each individual movement needed to create the given pose. Make sure to consider how much space each child may need in order to do the moves. As you all become more practiced at using yoga cards, the children may want to take the lead in modeling familiar poses, assisting peers in modifying their pose. Eventually, they may even suggest poses they create on their own.

Sustaining specific poses requires a great deal of balance and body awareness (Wolff & Stapp 2019). Using yoga cards allows you to observe children's strengths and consider the ways twos can be further challenged to support areas of emerging gross motor development. You can easily adapt this activity to increase or decrease difficulty, for example, by extending the time to hold a pose or modifying poses to be more inclusive of children's differing abilities. Consider doing seated yoga, which is a more inclusive option for children who use wheelchairs or might have difficulty sustaining poses while standing.

Summary

Children need variety and agency when moving their bodies. Offering diverse opportunities to stretch their skills and assess risk under careful supervision creates a deeper sense of trust with the child while meeting their changing needs. By engaging in collaborative decision-making with the child, you can celebrate these diverse needs and play approaches while fostering their confidence. You become an influential resource for the very young child, supporting their independent exploration of their evolving physical development as they build a repertoire of movement skills with appropriate play materials (Hadders-Algra 2010).

Suggested Play Materials

- Art materials (e.g., chunky brushes, crayons, markers, paper, scissors)
- Balls (e.g., large textured balls, lightweight balls with holes for grabbing)
- Beads for stringing
- Blocks (e.g., assorted wooden and cardboard blocks, BPA-free silicone blocks, bristle blocks, Magna-Tiles, Mega Bloks, mirror blocks)
- Buckets
- Cardboard tubes
- Cloth books
- Clutching toys (e.g., fabric-covered crinkly paper, interlocking rings, plastic keys, rattles, scarves, teethers)
- Cooking tools and supplies
- Cups
- Felt board with felt figures
- Funnels
- Nesting cups
- Objects with buckles, Velcro, and zippers
- Pegs of different colors and pegboards
- Playsets with movable characters and accessories
- Puzzles
- Sensory materials (e.g., clay, goop, grass, ice, mud, paint, playdough, sand, slime, soil, water)
- Shape sorters
- Shovels, scoops, and spoons
- Small characters (e.g., animals, people)
- Soft animals and textured fabrics (e.g., blankets, rugs)
- Sound exploration materials (e.g., flat river stones; instruments with handles; large spoons; metal objects like pots and pans; Ping-Pong balls on tile; rainsticks; sensory bottles with small objects like beads and buttons)
- Stacking toys
- Unbreakable bottles and containers with lids that can be pulled or screwed on and off
- Wooden bowls

CHAPTER 12

Play Materials That Enhance My Fine Motor Skills

This time in their lives is just a whisper, a brief moment, in which they can enjoy the richness of a childhood space.

—Bev Bos and Jenny Chapman, *Tumbling Over the Edge: A Rant for Children's Play*

Physical learning and development are deeply interwoven into each developmental domain, creating dynamic feedback loops among thinking, body awareness, feelings, and the ways in which children engage with the world around them socially. Young children usually develop motor skills from head to toes and proximal to distal (near to far). First the trunk (torso) and head stabilize, then shoulders, arms and legs, and finally hands and feet. Children need to have a stable base of gross motor (large muscle) function before they are ready to grasp and work toward isolating and developing the small muscles of their fingers and hands (i.e., fine motor skills).

As you consider the distinct ways in which young infants, mobile infants, toddlers, and twos manually examine and engage with the world, think about how you intentionally use materials in your learning space to support their growing and developing bodies. Each age group has its own process and focus for fine motor development, and simultaneously, each child has their own individualized needs and methods to engage their whole arm, whole hand, fingers, and pincer grasp (Huffman & Fortenberry 2011; NAEYC 2020).

The spontaneous and erratic movements of very young infants signal the beginning of the process of *body awareness*, the foundation of the ability to reach and grasp or engage more directly with the environment. Infants engage in pre-reaching movements, such as bumping their bodies or extending their limbs, as they try to engage the muscles needed to grasp and reach toward specific objects (Karl, Sacrey, & Whishaw 2018).

Slowly, as infants play with their hands, their movements become more intentional, and that intention is often to put things in their mouths. As Hadders-Algra (2018) acknowledged, "In the first 2–3 months after term, babies—like fetuses—direct about one-third or half of their hand movements to the face" (418). This is why it is so important during this phase of growth to provide safe materials for infants to mouth and in fact encourage them to mouth, allowing them to practice how to move and grasp while exploring. Keep bins nearby to store mouthed toys for sanitizing along with duplicate toys for replenishing materials as needed.

Soft Animals and Textured Fabrics

Before young infants have the ability to grasp objects independently, they primarily work with closed fists, exploring early gross motor reflexes as their bodies move and extend involuntarily. Over time, they build on their self-awareness and engage in more thorough investigations about how to direct their bodies' movements. Soft animals and fabrics are play materials that are safe, comforting, stimulating, and inviting for young infants.

To give young infants interesting touch sensations, place them on top of textured fabrics. This sensory experience is enhanced as they wiggle and move, glide their arms over a fuzzy blanket, or place a hand on top of a bumpy rug, pausing to gently squeeze it. Although their movements are still largely random, repetition of these experiences supports the refinement of their fine motor skills with whole-arm and whole-hand movements.

As the infant grows and begins exploring their surroundings more directly, provide safe materials they can easily grasp as they continue to build strength in their arms and hands. Soft plush animals are a safe play material to offer young infants as they continue to develop when and how to release materials they grasp, a skill they do not usually master until around 10 months.

Clutching Toys

Clutching toys are an assortment of play materials specifically chosen for young infants who are working on developing their *palmar grasp* (whole-hand grasp where the fingers move in toward the palm), which emerges from the palmar reflex and develops around the third month (Hadders-Algra 2018). You can observe this reflex by placing a finger in the palm of the baby's hand, which triggers an involuntary squeezing grasp from the child. Because young infants have not yet fully developed their upper body muscles and are still at the fundamental use of core muscles for balance and coordination, select clutching materials that are developmentally appropriate and safe. These include teethers, rattles, wooden rings, and certain types of balls.

Two key elements of clutching toys are that they have either moving parts or interesting textures. These materials intrigue young infants, who like to shake, move, and mouth them. Offer lightweight options that they can easily manipulate on their own without risk of injury as their arms and hands gain more stability.

Being such a versatile and multifunctional play material, balls truly should be a staple for any learning environment with very young children. In thinking about the development of fine motor skills in young infants, look for balls that can build muscles needed for grasping. Lightweight balls with holes encourage whole-hand engagement as children begin to explore their ability to transfer objects between their hands. These toys also support young infants' upper body development as they navigate their emerging grasping skills. As a young infant explores grasping and releasing, extend their play by catching and returning balls as they roll and move away from the child. Remember to pause, allowing them to visually track the ball and turn their body as needed to observe the unique way in which the ball rolls.

Mobile Infants (Discovery Seekers)

Continued development of gross motor skills allows mobile infants to begin exploring play materials with their simultaneously developing fine motor skills. You will notice that mobile infants have a greater sense of intentionality with their hands. Around 6 months, children begin to conduct experiments with objects, engaging in relatively long bouts of repetition and deeper exploration through which they discover the dynamic qualities of play materials and how best to manipulate them (Payne & Isaacs 2017). Allow mobile infants as much free time as possible to engage in this important activity.

Materials for Shaking

At about 7 months, mobile infants have typically refined the whole-hand grasping reflex to be able to grab items using their *pincer grasp* (where the index finger and thumb are pinched together). They begin to adapt their grasping techniques to suit the particular object they are trying to play with. This signals the transition into being able to multitask as they engage with play materials, engaging with objects using both hands at once while each one has a specific and different role. For instance, you might see a mobile infant hold a bell in one hand while carefully examining the texture or shape of the handle with the other (Kimmerle et al. 2010). This bimanual mobility will gradually become the primary method of object exploration, building muscles and dexterity (a more refined skill) in hands, which requires communication between both sides of the brain.

Play materials that allow experimentation with sound provide many opportunities for both hands to join in a unified task and are particularly important at this time. As mobile infants use both hands to bang two objects together, for instance, they begin to understand how they can move their bodies to create sound. Mobile infants love to discover this ability! Offer a variety of materials to bang and clang that make significant noise.

Allow mobile infants to investigate the properties of individual objects while building or refining their methods of manipulation and grasping techniques using one or both hands. You can support this investigation by offering large spaces and plenty of interesting objects for sound exploration and swapping out old materials for new ones once mobile infants seem to have lost interest. Try bells, sensory bottles filled with various small objects, or even a basket of metal bowls. Pay attention to what sounds mobile infants are comfortable with and explore other ways they might create similar sounds.

Stacking Rings, Nesting Cups, and Shape Sorters

Play materials such as stacking rings, nesting cups, and shape sorters offer experiences in grasping and releasing as a means of investigation. This repeated exercise strengthens hand–eye coordination, grasping techniques, and the ability to isolate specific fingers to

accomplish a goal. Offer these play materials on a low shelf, allowing nonwalkers easy access while seated. For an added challenge, offer this choice on a low shelf that also allows children who are working on standing the space to build and stack near the midline of their bodies. Start with simple grasp-and-release materials like small blocks or stacking rings. Add variety, such as beginning with lightweight nesting cups and slowly building toward heavier materials like wooden stackers as the child gains control and precision in their hands and fingers. Allow plenty of space for mobile infants to stack and sort without intervening, understanding that each attempt is part of the process and an important step in building strength and dexterity. Provide long stretches of discovery learning with unbreakable containers that have lids and small objects to place inside them. These experiences encourage children to understand how objects disappear and simultaneously build their fine motor skills while investigating.

Toddlers (Autonomy Seekers)

Toddlers are passionate people who feel a sense of urgency about learning to do things and be able to play in ways that are meaningful to them. Because of their higher level of self-awareness, they seek play materials that interest and challenge them and align with their need for self-discovery and autonomy (Payne & Isaacs 2017). The materials discussed in the following sections support toddlers' work on their small muscle development and pincer grasp.

Blocks

Mobile infants are naturally drawn toward block towers, primarily as a means to use their whole arm movements to excitedly knock them down. Although the love of knocking down a tall tower may not necessarily fade, toddlers may now become intrigued with the patience needed and decision-making processes involved in building a structure of their own. By about 15 months, toddlers become more capable at reaching, grasping, and releasing, and these skills are refined to the point that toddlers can begin stacking objects such as small blocks (Gerber, Wilks, & Erdie-Lalena 2010). As toddlers' skills begin to expand to allow them to grasp tightly or loosely, the types of structures they build will change.

One of the best ways to support this progression is to offer a variety of blocks. Keep in mind the capabilities and safety of the children when selecting blocks. Toddlers are usually not strong or coordinated enough to enjoy playing with large wooden blocks; however, there are many other kinds of blocks that would be appropriate. Some of these are classics (e.g., foam blocks, bristle blocks, lightweight cardboard blocks for larger structures), others are more recent materials and have interesting features (e.g., blocks with colored lenses and mirrors), and still others have updated safety features (e.g., squishy and firm BPA-free plastic blocks). Unit blocks, tree cookies and tree blocks, blocks that connect, and even Magna-Tiles offer a creative outlet for toddlers' fine motor skills and ability to problem solve in a hands-on manner.

Chunky Art Tools

Art materials should always be available for toddlers to engage their hands in creative problem solving and continue to refine their pincer grasp. As with any choice offered in learning environments, be mindful about the interests, abilities, and needs of the children in your group when considering what tools and experiences to offer. Provide tools that address their current abilities and needs as well as some that invite learning and new challenges.

As toddlers' pincer grasp continues to develop, offer art materials that are both easily grasped with open palms as well as those that can be manipulated with a transitional pincer grasp. Usually at around 18 months, toddlers are able to use their pincer grasp to hold a wide variety of tools they can use for drawing and scribbling visual art creations (Gerber, Wilks, & Erdie-Lalena 2010; see Chapter 9). Play materials such as chunky crayons, large paint brushes, playdough, large markers, large stamps and ink pads, bingo daubers, oil pastels, paint in squeeze bottles, and paper that can be crumpled and ripped provide many opportunities for toddlers to practice these emerging fine motor skills.

Sit with toddlers as they engage with the materials, making neutral observations and encouraging children's self-exploration. For example, you may say things like "Sylvie is squishing her dough, it's getting so flat," "Look, Kaysha, your finger made a tiny hole in your dough," and "Zeke, I see you're trying to roll your dough into a ball; your hands are moving back and forth so quickly!" Maintain pleasant conversations when they are relevant to the work of the children, but do not feel you have to fill every moment with chatter. Let everyone enjoy the quiet peace that so often accompanies intensely focused toddler work.

Twos (Identity Seekers)

Two-year-olds continue to refine and seek out mastery through more challenging fine motor experiences. What is distinctly different when comparing the busy work of toddlerhood with the focus of the 2-year-old is the ability of twos to weave attention and intention into their play. Two-year-olds begin to approach their work with specific goals, having the ability to recall previous experiences. These goals, of course, may change throughout play, but more often twos seek out choices that allow them to build confidence in their skills and create a sense of order.

Art Materials with Props

As mentioned in the previous section for toddlers, art experiences are a wonderful venue for young children to engage their hands and fingers in creative pursuits. As twos gain increasing control, precision, and grasping ability through practice, they engage with art materials in new ways. As the foundational fine motor skills to complete tasks are becoming easier, twos' focus shifts toward using these skills to make their ideas come to life, bringing their own personal touch to the experience.

Although both toddlers and 2-year-olds use art materials (e.g., paper, clay, playdough), identity-seeking twos use these materials not only as an exploratory experience but also as a way to define their unique perspectives. Support this desire by offering art materials that encourage mixing, blending, adding, and the combining of mediums (e.g., paint, glue, markers, clay). A 2-year-old is looking for ways to create their own story line—their sense of self—and will weave in details to any area of their work.

Offer 2-year-olds trays to contain their work, which also helps in establishing boundaries with the work of surrounding peers. Cups of paint, cotton balls, pieces of tissue paper, colored sand, pom-poms, and craft feathers encourage decision-making and unique creative expression. Allow children to select the materials they want and add details to their work as they see fit. Provide a variety of tools, such as thick brushes, craft sticks, corks, sponges, and stamps to change the process of their work and encourage them to engage with art materials in new ways. These tools can also make art experiences more accessible to children with sensory sensitivities. When work is completed, make sure to display the children's art in a space that is at their eye level, allowing them to review and examine their own work and that of their peers.

Playsets with Movable Characters and Accessories

When nurturing the imaginative play of 2-year-olds, remember it is about the journey and not necessarily the destination. Sometimes the preparation or setting of the scene for a play scenario becomes the primary objective for twos. They use fine motor skills throughout this process as they position play materials, gather supplies, and create scenes that often depict experiences from their own lives. No matter what scenario the child has in mind, such play encourages fine motor development while also offering a way to add depth to storytelling.

When offering materials for 2-year-olds to create play scenes, organize loose parts and scenery pieces to support their decision-making process. Keep baskets moderately full and clearly labeled with both pictures as well as words so the child knows what supplies are being offered. Represent children's home languages by offering labels in multiple languages. Add props that are relevant to the children's daily lives and supplement them over time, adding materials that represent their interests, languages, cultures, and families. Enhance the use of more concrete scenes (e.g., doll house, grocery store, hospital, car garage) by offering a variety of contextual props (e.g., doll furniture, shopping cart, ambulance, small cars).

Such scenes are enhanced when twos have access to natural materials and other various loose parts. These might include empty recycled containers, small stones, blocks of different sizes, felt pieces cut into various shapes, cardboard tubes, or any small component that might inspire twos to personalize their scenes. The greater the variety of props and materials accessible to twos, the more challenged they will be to use and develop different fine motor movements. The more thoroughly involved 2-year-olds are with these materials, the longer their engagement becomes and the more opportunities they will have to practice their emerging fine motor skills.

Infants and Toddlers at Play

Summary

During the first three years, young children refine their fine motor skills, starting with their arms, their hands, and eventually their fingers. Over time, very young children build strength, precision, dexterity, and body awareness as they find new ways to engage with the world around them. The materials in this chapter support young children at each step of this journey. Consider the children's interests, abilities, languages, cultures, and families when you select materials that can inspire and strengthen the process of fine motor mastery.

Suggested Play Materials

- Baby carriers and slings
- Backpacks filled with heavy materials
- Balance beams, boards, and seats
- Body pillows
- Cardboard boxes to climb in (e.g., major appliance boxes)
- Hammocks (cloth and low-hanging)
- Hula-Hoops
- Large trucks
- Music to move, dance, and bounce to
- Playdough and clay
- Pop-up tents
- Rocking chairs and yoga balls
- Ropes to pull (tied to a fence or doorknob)
- Teeter-totters
- Tunnels
- Velcro on felt boards
- Sensory socks filled with materials (e.g., crunchy leaves, jingle bells, sand, sponges)
- Stress balls
- Strollers, buggies, and wagons
- Swings and other things to swing on
- Washed milk jugs filled with water for carrying
- Weighted jugs

CHAPTER 13

Play Materials That Teach Me About My Body in Space

If we provide enough space and possibilities for moving freely, then the children will move as well as animals: skillfully, simply, securely, naturally.

—Emmi Pikler, *Peaceful Babies—Contented Mothers (Mit tud már a baba?)*

Two aspects of physical learning and development—those involving large and small muscles—are what we usually think of first when considering children's physical development. This chapter dives deeper, looking at how very young children develop and learn balance (vestibular system) and how their bodies and parts of their bodies move through space (proprioception).

The vestibular system, located in the inner ear, is a major regulatory hub that helps us to establish our sense of balance and understand whether or not our bodies or our surroundings are in motion. It develops throughout the child's life as a mechanism to establish appropriate balance and motor management needed in various postures (Archer & Siraj 2015).

Proprioception works as a partner to the vestibular system. Located in our joints, muscles, and tendons, this feedback system sends signals to the brain, deciphering the location of body parts in space and providing specific information regarding the movements of isolated body parts like the arms or legs. These qualities typically involve sensations such as tight, loose, wobbly, fast, slow, or various forms of pressure on the body as it stretches and bends.

The proprioception system of feedback in very young children allows them to move safely within a space, and it works hand in hand with their vestibular system to help their bodies maintain posture, coordinate movement patterns, and strengthen muscle tone. In other words, in order for children's bodies to move successfully, they need to develop a strong sense of proprioception to coordinate how and when which body parts need to move. The more opportunities a child has to move their body, particularly engaging freely in the environment through play, the more information their central nervous system receives, which in turn engages the child's vestibular system and sense of proprioception. This system of movement information and coordination continues to grow and develop through adulthood.

Young Infants (Security Seekers)

Young infants build awareness of their moving bodies and how they engage with the surrounding space through joint engagement with you. Moving with the infant allows them to develop their own sense of movement and coordination from a place of secure attachment. Young infants begin to use their vestibular sense through visual tracking and observing and identifying motion around their bodies. As they slowly begin to develop muscle tone in the trunk of their bodies, even the slightest head movement can send a variety of signals to the brain. Similarly, young infants begin to develop their proprioceptive sense through direct contact with you during care routines. The way you move young infants matters, and the opportunities you provide for them to move their own bodies continue to lay the foundation for the child's entire motor functioning.

Strollers and Buggies

In the hustle and bustle of an infant space, going on a buggy walk becomes quite an enjoyable experience for young infants. Focusing specifically on the vestibular system and proprioceptive processing, strollers or buggies offer young infants the opportunity to observe their own movement as they adjust to the speed of the buggy increasing and decreasing as well as changes in direction. Before moving outdoors, make sure your safety equipment is in proper working order (parts such as buckles, straps, and supportive gear) to keep children comfortably and safely seated throughout your walk. Consider packing a small bag with items that may further offer comfort, like sun hats, tissues, and weather-appropriate layers, as needed.

At every stop, the young infant's vestibular system adapts and experiences a rush of sensory information. To the child with sensory sensitivity, these slight adjustments in the inner ear might cause them to feel as though they are on a small roller coaster. Accordingly, adjust your movements to match children's characteristics and needs, perhaps gently stopping every so often to allow the child to adapt while you closely observe them. For some children, this may be soothing and comforting, while others with higher sensitivity may find this sensation to be quite concerning. Stay attuned to the expressions and emotions of the young infants you are with so you can create movement experiences that are informed, individualized, and inviting.

In the stroller or buggy, most young infants will ease back into their seats and enjoy observing the world around them. This simple activity facilitates their understanding that they are separate—and moving—persons who are distinct from the objects they see. These moments of deep relaxation and sensory regulation are wonderful times to sing familiar songs to young infants. Engage them in meaningful conversations about what they feel, see, and hear as you follow their cues about what interests them.

Rocking Chairs and Yoga Balls

Feeding and sleeping are two care routines that take precedence as young infants' bodies begin to regulate their own natural schedules. Emotional regulation is also important, as discussed in earlier chapters. Rocking chairs and yoga balls are important tools for soothing young infants as they experience a variety of sensory input in your learning space, both external (e.g., loud sounds or bright lights) and internal (e.g., feeling their own hunger cues or the discomfort that comes with needing a diaper change).

While seated in a rocking chair or glider with a young infant in your arms and enjoying the back-and-forth rhythm together, exchange facial expressions and babbles. Discuss anything that has caught the child's attention as you stay attuned to the comfort of the child. Some young infants enjoy lying back with their neck supported on your arm; others may prefer sitting more upright against your body, with your supportive hand on their abdomen.

Yoga balls can also be used for soothing experiences. Sit with your feet firmly planted on the ground and the child safely held in your arms. Gently bounce or sway, perhaps to music playing in the background or your own quiet humming or singing. Yoga balls can be a wonderful addition to any early learning space because they not only provide new types of movement for the child, they are also a physical support for you as you facilitate children's exploration.

Mobile Infants (Discovery Seekers)

As young infants become independently mobile, active play and exploration of the environment allow their brains to collect more data about how their bodies are moving (i.e., developing their proprioceptive sense) and how to balance (i.e., developing their vestibular sense). Even seemingly simple activities like sitting involve complex brain–body dialogue between muscle coordination and strength, balance, and stability (Adolph & Robinson 2015). It is important during this phase of development that mobile infants have opportunities to explore and move at their own pace, honoring the natural progression of motor development that unfolds at its own time, in its own way, at its own pace (NAEYC 2020).

The vestibular system and proprioceptive sense constantly work in the background in ways that are difficult to see. There is a world of sensations the child is experiencing under the surface. With this in mind, the play materials discussed in the following sections encourage discovery learning that engages mobile infants' body awareness and balance.

Tunnels

As mobile infants venture out into the world, they are naturally curious about it. Mobile infants find endless ways to experiment with risk as they continue to define and redefine their physical limits. Tunnels are wonderful additions that encourage discovery learning and multisensory communication to the brain. "Crawling on hands and knees combines balance, vision, touch, and proprioception" (Archer & Siraj 2015, 17). Using a tunnel creates an

additional proprioceptive experience as the child pushes forward through the tunnel. Their brain senses the boundaries of their bodies in relation to the tunnel walls and calculates the distance to the exit.

To support mobile infants as they explore tunnels, allow each child the opportunity to explore in ways that feel comfortable to them. Some children may want to sit and touch the tunnel on the outside, noticing how it feels as it resists when they push on it with their hands. Other children may feel ready to crawl inside immediately. You may observe a mobile infant who, while trying to crawl through, stops midway and looks concerned, possibly worrying that they are stuck or maybe feeling a bit claustrophobic. Position yourself so that you are in constant eyesight of the child, adding security as they explore. If a child is more hesitant to enter the tunnel, try gently rolling a ball inside or simply place an arm or hand inside so that they can observe this depth of movement. If a child gets worried or frustrated while inside the tunnel, calmly encourage them to crawl forward or extend a helping hand if they need further assistance. Stay calm and allow the infant to openly explore the tunnel when they are ready.

Allow the opportunity for mobile infants to problem solve with their bodies and notice they are not able to move in the same ways while in the tunnel that they are in open space. They may need to go around a friend's body or perhaps reposition themselves to create more space for themselves or a peer. This type of problem solving and peer engagement is unique to materials like tunnels, which is part of their major appeal to teachers, who like the endless play dynamics they create.

Squishy, Squeezy, and Flexible Materials

During mobile infancy, the child experiences so much development and change in all domains, but nowhere is it more apparent than in their physical growth. As mobile infants begin to move throughout their environments, opportunities that facilitate proprioception become increasingly important as they start to study their own movement. Providing this age group with dynamic play materials that allow them to integrate their whole bodies into play nourishes a deeper understanding of awareness of self, how bodies move, and the sensations that happen in movement.

When considering play materials that support body awareness, provide a variety of experiences that allow the child to experiment with how much pressure they are comfortable with and wish to engage in. In Chapter 11, we discussed firm proprioceptive climbing materials such as a loft, but there are many other options that mobile infants can use. Such materials allow them to squeeze, push, and press against various body parts as they explore materials such as low-hanging cloth hammocks, beanbags, large cardboard boxes to climb in and out of, pop-up tents, body pillows, stress balls, and sensory socks (filled with materials like sand, jingle bells, sponges, and small toys). When making sensory socks, place the materials in one sock, tie it securely, put this first sock into a second sock, and tie it closed with another tight knot.

Toddlers (Autonomy Seekers)

Toddlers are still experimenting to understand the size and capabilities of their bodies. You might find a toddler trying to wear a doll hat, wanting to sit in a tiny basket, trying to lift a blanket they are standing on, or becoming frustrated when they are unable to do the same things they see adults do. The play materials featured in the following sections focus on supporting autonomy-seeking toddlers in this growing sense of bodily awareness and suggest a variety of experiences for toddlers in the pursuit of independence.

Materials That Can Be Pushed or Pulled or Give Resistance

As toddlers seek experiences that give them more information about their own bodies, offer play materials they can push and move. Toddlers who are beginning to take steps and transition into walking love using different types of push toys. These might include large lightweight trucks, small chairs, buggies and strollers, large balls, and walkers that can help toddlers pull up to stand, take their first steps, and then push around the setting.

Toddlers begin to objectively see their bodies as a major component of play or a tool for accomplishing a task they wish to pursue. They are all about using their bodies for trial-and-error problem solving (Brownell, Zerwas, & Ramani 2007). To understand their bodies, toddlers need to define their own limitations and physical capabilities through repetitive play research. Pushing and making contact with heavier materials adds pressure and resistance to physical tasks, engaging both the balance established in the vestibular system as well as the proprioceptive sense of body awareness. The child also begins to observe their own body in motion as they make things move.

Safe play materials that offer heavier pressure when pushed can continue to challenge toddlers who need even more sensory stimulation and proprioceptive information. For this, provide wagons that peers are able to climb in and out of and that another toddler pushes and navigates. If they are not comfortable sharing this experience with a peer, encourage them to load their cart with heavy objects such as blocks or weighted sensory bags. Pull toys offer a different experience, allowing the child to cross their midline while utilizing upper body muscles to pull against the wagon (the resistance) behind their body. There are a variety of pull toys on the market including animals or trucks on wheels with a string attached, wagons with handles, or walking toys that create sound as they move.

Materials for Balancing

As toddlers begin to master walking, offer play materials to help them practice balance. Materials that are low to the ground create play experiences that require the joint efforts of muscle control, proprioceptive awareness, balance, and risk assessment. Essentially, these play materials provide physical challenges for toddlers that are different from stable and familiar flat surfaces, adding new dimensions of problem solving. With each step, they need to stabilize their gaze, find control in their posture, focus on the sensations of their feet getting grounded against the new surface, and feel the edges in order to position and reposition their core center of balance.

Toddlers can pursue these balancing experiences using a variety of materials both indoors and outdoors. For instance, you can line up a collection of large wooden blocks, creating dynamic shapes for the children to walk over. Foam balance beams offer a similar experience with a different texture. Have toddlers take off their shoes for this experience to stimulate the soles of their feet. In the outdoor play yard, provide logs and small climbing stones for a novel experience with climbing or balancing.

Support young toddlers' emerging climbing skills by positioning your body close to the child. Remain calm and present, talking through moments of fear, apprehension, or frustration with encouraging language. Allow children time to problem solve on their own while giving physical cues that support their safety. Rather than simply saying "Be careful," you might offer more concrete feedback, such as "Slow your body. Do you feel safe? If you feel wobbly, bring your body closer to the ground." Remember, the goal of climbing and balancing is not to prevent falling but rather to create an inviting and safe environment for the child to experience falling in a way in which they will not be hurt. Falling or losing balance is an important part of the learning process. This by no means suggests you should remain on the sideline watching; be closely involved in the child's exploration through body positioning and available to provide more direct feedback if needed.

Twos (Identity Seekers)

Two-year-olds continue to investigate autonomous thought shaped throughout their toddlerhood. Taking it a step further, twos begin to understand how they are different from other people, with their own distinct thoughts, voices, bodies, and approaches to learning. Their autonomous efforts deepen from the fundamental need to do things on their own toward more complex decision-making, problem solving, and forms of physical expression. As Brownell, Zerwas, and Ramani (2007) said, "because this means imagining oneself from a third-person perspective, it also, interestingly, provides the wherewithal to begin to use one's own body deliberately as a tool and to manipulate or alter one's body as a means of personal expression" (1438). This emerging form of exploration and understanding of self is shaped even further as new methods of collaborative play become the primary form of relating to others. The materials discussed in this section allow twos to experiment with their individuality as they engage in collaborative motor play.

Music to Move, Dance, and Bounce To

As discussed in earlier chapters, sharing music together can be a wonderfully connecting and collaborative experience for 2-year-olds. Through musical activities, they fully engage their balance and body awareness in fun and enjoyable ways. As you begin to incorporate more opportunities for twos to make their own decisions, movement with music can become a powerful opportunity for children to make active choices about their bodies and begin to coordinate their own motor planning.

Introduce a variety of genres and diverse artists to the children, moving along with them as they investigate how each song might feel with expressive movement. Select artists and genres that reflect the cultures of each child and their family, asking families what they enjoy listening to at home. Highlight the movements of each child, pinpointing how each child's movement is different and unique. You can add strong descriptive words to this activity (e.g., *bouncy, smooth, slow, fast, light, heavy*) and discuss what areas of their bodies children are moving.

Songs with directions do more than just assist twos with listening and executing appropriate planning; they provide a challenge to isolate and locate specific body parts, experiment with speed or varying degrees of pressure, and explore motor combinations they may not have tried on their own. Add props such as scarves and musical instruments or combine movement with a storytelling experience to extend and inspire further creativity in movement. Use music during transition times in the classroom, adding enjoyment and familiar cues to support children as they clean up and prepare for a meal or move outdoors. These playful yet challenging experiences continuously bathe the child in sensory information as they reorient their center of balance through play and establish their dynamic relationship between their body and space.

Obstacle Courses

As 2-year-olds are driven by their need to develop a sense of identity, it is important to provide materials that offer opportunities to show their individuality in play. Overcoming an obstacle takes trial-and-error problem solving, determination, patience, vulnerability, and at times, having the necessary social skills to ask for help. These valuable parts of a growing sense of self can all be practiced and researched through motor play, specifically as the child navigates obstacle courses.

Obstacle courses can be created with a variety of materials, such as those listed throughout the chapter, providing new sensory stimulation at each point in the experience. Create a route that calls for a variety of movement patterns, switching between hopping, tiptoeing, climbing, crawling, rolling, and balancing. Once a child has finished the obstacle course, encourage them to start over again. With each time through it, a child brings more experience and knowledge to the task, building confidence in their physical capabilities as well as their ability to solve problems on their own. As 2-year-olds plan how they need to move their body to get up a ramp or delight in the challenge of having to transition from crawling to hopping, there are many ways proprioception and the vestibular system are engaged. Specifically, twos need to utilize bilateral movement, sensory stimulation, agility, coordination, spatial awareness, directionality, positionality, and balance to solve these body puzzles.

Set up obstacle courses using materials that offer different sensory experiences, highlighting a variety of motor skills. Consider materials such as stepping-stones (e.g., rubber circle mats or even textured mats), tunnels, balance beams, cones, traffic signs, Hula-Hoops, pillows, and platforms. These courses can be a collaborative effort, planned by you and the children. Twos can assist in setting up the areas or make suggestions for what types of movement they would like to try. These experiences should be inviting and developmentally appropriate, allowing twos to choose which areas they want to focus on and which they do not feel ready to explore.

Summary

Over the course of this chapter, we discussed how engaging the vestibular system while supporting proprioception supports very young learners as they begin to explore and experiment with their changing bodies. This allows them to connect with themselves, each other, and the world around them. As children grow and develop, the role of their bodies in play changes. Children who feel capable and confident in their bodies are willing to take risks, face new experiences with excitement, problem solve to meet changing conditions, and find an inner strength that defines them and their sense of self.

In Your Words

Jennifer Addleman and Samantha Sisk, co-lead teachers from Indiana University's Campus View Child Care Center in Bloomington, Indiana, share their thoughts about supporting physical development, learning, and well-being in children from birth to age 3.

. . . .

With every new group of children, we carefully curate an environment that provides children with opportunities for exploration and experimentation of their minds and bodies. When we support children's physical learning and development (large motor, small motor, and balance and understanding of how the body moves in space), we know that it also impacts their development in other areas. As we set up the room, we think about the abilities and interests of the children in our group. We design and adapt the environment with each community of children in mind, modifying the selection of materials available, the physical layout, and the tone of the class (e.g., whether low-key and calm or upbeat and exciting) to best fit the ever-changing abilities and interests of the children. We provide materials that enable children to practice and refine what they know how to do and that also encourage the children to learn and develop through scaffolding. The outdoor environment is a mirror of the indoor space. Materials we value offer multilevel learning opportunities, are made from natural materials, have a variety of textures, and represent children's everyday life, including their cultures, languages, and families.

With infants, we foster free movement and exploration. Infants are encouraged to be active participants, always free to move where they wish. We carefully set up the room to encourage natural development such as rolling over, pulling up, crawling, and then walking. We have a small loft that works their upper body, encourages risk-taking, allows them to learn about their bodies in relationship to others as well as in space, and finally, builds problem-solving skills. We also use such items as wooden baby play gyms, a mirrored and carpeted crawl-through tunnel, risers, and everyday materials such as snack containers with lids for children to manipulate.

As toddlers and twos, the children have more advanced opportunities to build and hone their skills. We expand our loft to include a tunnel, ramp, and slide. Other materials include tubes with loose parts, a variety of blocks (e.g., DUPLO blocks, large hollow blocks, cube blocks that fit in one hand), weighted balls, beanbags for throwing, beads for stringing, and a variety of wooden early STEM materials, such as stackers, stringers, and puzzles.

Even with all of the planning and opportunities we provide, we also make changes to meet the interests and abilities of the children. Several years ago, we had a group of children who loved to climb. They had advanced their skills beyond the physical materials that were available, including climbing over the side of the loft onto the windowsill. We brainstormed and came up with an idea. We had a low shelf at the center that was no longer needed and decided to bring it into the room and laid it flat on the floor for the children to climb in and out of. We padded it around the edges with old sit-upons so the children could safely climb in and out without the fear of hitting their heads or splinters. This idea was such a hit that we eventually purchased padding and fabric to upholster the shelf. The result was a new opportunity and space for children to climb as well as use their climbing skills in a different way. This material also invited imaginative play (it became a bus, a rowboat, a train, and more). The children seemed to enjoy that they could also climb into tiny "safe spaces" that they could have all to themselves while still being part of the group.

Final Thoughts

In this book, we presented the who, why, how, and what of play materials for young infants, mobile infants, toddlers, and twos. We featured materials specifically suited to meet the dynamic interests, abilities, and needs of these very young children as they grow and develop; support them holistically; and honor their individual interests, abilities, and preferences (NAEYC 2020). Play materials and your understanding about how very young children experience them are important in helping them live each day to its fullest (i.e., focus on their *being*) and preparing them to meet the future (i.e., focus on their *becoming*).

It is our hope that we have provided information and ideas that will spark ongoing conversations, inspire you to be fully mindful and responsive in your interactions with the very young children in your learning community, encourage you to be intentional when you plan learning environments and experiences, and help you further recognize and appreciate infants and toddlers as wonderfully capable human beings.

Appendix A

Highlights of Learning, Development, and Positive Well-Being

Young Infants (Birth to About 6 Months)

Primary Focus: Security | I am one with the environment.

Cognitive Learning, Development, and Well-Being

I learn how things work.

I learn about how the world works.

I like to look around and see new and different people and things.

I explore with both my hands and my mouth.

I smoothly follow toys that move across my field of vision.

I focus on toys and things just out of reach and reach for them.

I seek out patterns.

I am drawn to faces and enjoy seeing and hearing other children.

I perform simple actions and begin to notice when something happens.

I see that others can make things happen by acting on objects.

I learn crying gets someone to come to me.

Social and Emotional Learning, Development, and Well-Being

I learn who I am and how I feel.

I don't recognize that I'm a separate being from other objects and people.

I enjoy seeing all the people and things around me but lack a sense of self.

I learn to trust your love and like to be with you.

I feel secure when you hold me.

I learn to comfort myself.

I like to suck my fingers or hands; it makes me feel good and safe.

I like to talk with you.

I smile, you smile back; you speak, and I make sounds in response.

I show early signs of empathy.

I cry when I hear others cry, called *contagious crying*.

Physical Learning, Development, and Well-Being

I learn how to move and do.

At first, reflexes make my body move automatically.

I search for something to suck.

I turn my head when breathing is blocked.

Later, I use my fingers, hands, feet, and legs to get things done.

I can move objects from hand to hand.

I put my hand and objects in my mouth.

I can kick a mobile and it moves; after a time, I learn to kick it on purpose.

I stretch my arms toward you to be picked up.

I learn to move with purpose.

I use my body to begin conveying my emotions and expressing my needs.

I roll over back to front.

Adapted from and informed by CDE (2009), Lally (2008), McMullen (2013), and NRC & IOM (2000)

Mobile Infants (About 6–8 Months to 12–15 Months)

Primary Focus: Discovery | I am in an environment with other people and things.

Cognitive Learning, Development, and Well-Being

I learn how things work.

I learn more about my world.

I like to play peekaboo.

I repeat the actions that I find enjoyable or that cause a reaction.

I recognize and remember things that are done routinely and anticipate them.

I am becoming a problem solver.

I increasingly use vocalizations and gestures to get help with things.

I can focus on an object or activity for a few minutes at a time.

I like to put things into containers and then dump them out into piles.

I can find objects that are hidden if I still see part of it peeking out.

I explore the attributes of objects.

I study language.

I find enjoyment in singing beloved songs with you.

I practice naming familiar objects and people in play.

Social and Emotional Learning, Development, and Well-Being

I learn who I am and how I feel.

I begin to recognize that other people behave and look differently.

I am curious about others and drawn to what they are doing.

I am an onlooker most of the time, sometimes imitating what others are doing but not partnering with them.

I begin to babble and desire to be part of conversation.

I still need to feel secure as I venture forth and explore.

I need to refuel physically by getting a hug now and then or by making eye contact with you.

I am becoming more empathetic.

I mimic facial expressions and imitate helping behaviors I've seen before.

I notice when others need help.

Physical Learning, Development, and Well-Being

I learn how to move and do.

I learn to move my whole body to go places and do things.

I can roll around in all directions—back to front, front to back.

I start creeping, scooting, and then crawling to get where I want to go.

I pull myself up to stand, holding on to something for support.

I cruise along furniture and walls, standing on my own two feet or walking by holding on to your hands.

I can sit up by myself for several minutes at a time.

I use my pincer grasp to pick up very small things.

I can feed myself by hand.

I use my hands to mimic gestures I have observed in conversation and explore how to use my body to communicate (e.g., clapping).

I can use simple sign language to express physical needs, such as *eat* and *milk*.

Adapted from and informed by CDE (2009), Lally (2008), McMullen (2013), and NRC & IOM (2000)

Toddlers (About 10–14 Months to 24 Months)

Primary Focus: Autonomy | I am a person.

Cognitive Learning, Development, and Well-Being

I learn how things work.

I continue to learn about the world.

I combine two simple actions and make things happen.

I am beginning to experiment with things to see how they respond.

I am a sponge for language and begin exploring schemas in how I identify objects and people.

I solve simple problems with trial and error and my sensorimotor skills.

I can now use objects as tools.

I can watch someone else solve a problem and then repeat it myself.

I understand when objects are similar and when they are different.

I can sort objects into two groups.

I can find objects that are completely hidden if I see someone hide them.

I begin to predict daily routines through familiar verbal cues.

I understand one object can represent another.

I enjoy pretending, like using a block as a phone, rocking a baby doll, and dressing up as someone else.

Social and Emotional Learning, Development, and Well-Being

I learn who I am and how I feel.

I am a person.

I know the baby in the mirror is me.

I now understand that I am a person, like the others I see; I'm one of them.

I count on you for clear and consistent limits to keep me safe.

When I test limits, I am learning who I am and how I should behave.

My feelings can be very strong and conflicting.

I sometimes feel frustrated because I cannot express my feelings verbally.

Sometimes I push you away; other times I need you to hold me close.

My empathy is continuing to develop.

I now pat the back of a crying friend or bring them their favorite toy.

I learn how to care for others by the way you care for me.

I begin using language as a tool to connect with peers in brief moments of collaborative play.

I appreciate when trusted adults help me verbally process my feelings when I am calm and secure.

Physical Learning, Development, and Well-Being

I learn how to move and do.

I can walk all by myself.

I can also run, but I may be unsteady.

I begin to assess risk as I move.

I love to dance and move my body to music, by myself or in groups.

I can transition between my movements with greater ease.

I use my hands more intentionally.

I isolate one finger to point.

I begin to multitask with both hands.

I love fingerplays and to clap along to songs.

I use my hands to put things together and take them apart.

I become aware of the space around me and use my body to problem solve and accomplish things.

I love scribbling using my entire arm and upper body.

I love swinging and moving in space.

My expressive language becomes clearer and more pronounced.

I begin to name my body parts.

Adapted from and informed by CDE (2009), Lally (2008), McMullen (2013), and NRC & IOM (2000)

Twos (About 18–24 Months to 36 Months)

Primary Focus: Identity | I am this person.

Cognitive Learning, Development, and Well-Being

I learn how things work.

I learn how the world works.

I have a strong sense of cause and effect and use it to accomplish goals.

I can hypothesize and predict what might happen in the future.

I ask questions as I problem solve and make meaning of the world around me.

I begin to read familiar books aloud or create my own stories by looking at the pictures.

I begin to think about how to solve simple problems.

I no longer have to physically try different solutions; now I can manipulate ideas in my mind.

I remember what I've tried before that has worked and do it again.

I can sort and organize things into multiple groupings.

I know where toys and books are kept and will look for missing ones.

I love dramatic play with others.

I can take on a role and pretend.

Social and Emotional Learning, Development, and Well-Being

I learn who I am and how I feel.

I know that I am a particular, special person that others love and care for.

I know I like certain things, for things to be a certain way, and that others might think differently.

I feel good about myself when my culture, language, and family are reflected in the setting.

I feel I belong when you speak in my home language and feel proud when I see photos of my family and people who look like me.

Storytelling is interwoven into my play, and I enjoy expressing my ideas to others.

My feelings are very strong, but I'm learning to control them.

I am learning to use my words to express how I feel.

I know more about what you expect of me.

My empathy is continuing to develop; I know others have feelings too.

I get concerned when my friends are sad, hurt, or need an adult's attention.

Physical Learning, Development, and Well-Being

I learn how to move and do.

I move my body with intention and more precision.

I begin to gain more control with my hands and fingers.

I enjoy physical tasks that require more focus, such as cutting with scissors or sculpting with clay.

I can build structures of varying heights and sizes.

I may use one hand to hold an object and the other to explore it fully.

I am curious about body language and explore different ways I can use my body to show you how I feel.

I seek out physical choices that use my whole body, such as jumping, dancing, or riding a bike.

I often enjoy rough-and-tumble play with supervision.

I have a stronger sense of balance.

I can climb up and down stairs alone.

Adapted from and informed by CDE (2009), Lally (2008), McMullen (2013), and NRC & IOM (2000)

Appendix B

On the Bookshelf

Part Two: Cognitive Learning and Development (Chapters 5–7)

Help Me Construct Knowledge and Understanding

- *Baby Up, Baby Down: A First Book of Opposites*, by Abrams Appleseed

- *Clap Hands*, by Helen Oxenbury

- *Hush! A Thai Lullaby*, by Minfong Ho, illustrated by Holly Meade

- *Little You*, by Richard Van Camp, illustrated by Julie Flett

- *My Up and Down and All Around Book*, by Marjorie W. Pitzer

- *Peekaboo Morning*, by Rachel Isadora

- *Say Hello!* by Rachel Isadora

- *Ten, Nine, Eight*, by Molly Bang

Facilitate My Thinking and Problem-Solving Skills

- *Baby Says*, by John Steptoe

- *Brown Bear, Brown Bear, What Do You See?* by Bill Martin Jr., illustrated by Eric Carle

- *Counting on Community*, by Innosanto Nagara

- *Green Is a Chile Pepper: A Book of Colors*, by Roseanne Greenfield Thong, illustrated by John Parra

- *The Little Mouse, the Red Strawberry, and the Big Hungry Bear*, by Don and Audrey Wood, illustrated by Don Wood

- *Round Is a Mooncake: A Book of Shapes*, by Roseanne Thong, illustrated by Grace Lin

- *So Far Up*, by Susanne Strasser

- *What Will Fit?* by Grace Lin

Inspire My Approaches to Learning

- *Chicka Chicka Boom Boom*, by Bill Martin Jr. and John Archambault, illustrated by Lois Ehlert

- *Dream Big, Little Leader*, by Vashti Harrison

- *Five Little Ducks*, illustrated by Penny Ives

- *Homemade Love*, by bell hooks, illustrated by Shane W. Evans

- *I Can Do It Too!* by Karen Baicker, illustrated by Ken Wilson-Max

- *I Like Berries, Do You?* by Marjorie W. Pitzer

- *Please, Baby, Please*, by Spike Lee and Tonya Lewis Lee, illustrated by Kadir Nelson

- *Shades of Black: A Celebration of Our Children*, by Sandra L. Pinkney, photographs by Myles C. Pinkney

- *You Are Extraordinary*, by Craig and Samantha Johnson, illustrated Sally Garland

Part Three: Social and Emotional Learning and Development (Chapters 8–10)

Help Me Understand Myself and Others

- *Baby Faces: A Book of Happy, Silly, Funny Faces*, by Amy Pixton, illustrated by Kate Merritt

- *Daddy, Papa, and Me*, by Lesléa Newman, illustrated by Carol Thompson

- *Dim Sum for Everyone!* by Grace Lin

- *Everywhere Babies,* by Susan Meyers, illustrated by Marla Frazee

- *Global Babies*, by the Global Fund for Children

- *I Am Latino: The Beauty in Me*, by Sandra L. Pinkney, photographs by Myles C. Pinkney

- *Mommy, Momma, and Me*, by Lesléa Newman, illustrated by Carol Thompson

- *My Parts Equal Me!* by Beverly C. Heath, illustrated by John Floyd Jr.

- *Special People, Special Ways*, by Arlene Maguire, illustrated by Sheila Bailey

Encourage Me to Express Myself Creatively

- *Baby Beluga*, by Raffi, illustrated by Ashley Wolff

- *Bronxtones*, by Alex Rivera

- *Dancing Feet!* by Lindsey Craig, illustrated by Marc Brown

- *Farmyard Beat*, by Lindsey Craig, illustrated by Marc Brown

- *Freight Train*, by Donald Crews

- *Little Naturalists: John James Audubon Painted Birds*, by Kate Coombs, illustrated by Seth Lucas

- *Pantone: Colors*, by Pantone

- *The Snowman*, by Raymond Briggs

- *The Snowy Day*, by Ezra Jack Keats

- *You Are My Sunshine*, by Jimmie Davis, illustrated by Caroline Jayne Church

Connect Me to Nature and Science

- *Black Bear, Red Fox: Colours in Cree*, by Julie Flett

- *City Critters*, by Antonia Banyard

- *I Love You, Sun, I Love You, Moon*, by Karen Pandell, illustrated by Tomie dePaolo

- *If You Plant a Seed*, by Kadir Nelson

- *Let's Go Outside!* by Ekaterina Trukhan

- *Little Bitty Friends*, by Elizabeth McPike, illustrated by Patrice Barton

- *Look and Learn* series (*Bugs, Birds, Baby Animals,* and others), by National Geographic Kids

- *Nature: Early Learning at the Museum*, by Nosy Crow and the British Museum

- *Rain!* by Linda Ashman, illustrated by Christian Robinson

- *Smithsonian Kids: A Walk in the Forest*, by Jaye Garnett, illustrated by Lisa Manuzak

- *Sweetest Kulu*, by Celina Kalluk, illustrated by Alexandria Neonakis

- *Up to My Knees!* by Grace Lin

Part Four: Physical Learning and Development (Chapters 11–13)

Help Me Develop My Gross Motor Skills

- *All Fall Down*, by Helen Oxenbury

- *Baby Dance*, by Ann Taylor, illustrated by Marjorie van Heerden

- *Busy Toes*, by C.W. Bowie, illustrated by Fred Willingham

- *Dance!* by Bill T. Jones and Susan Kuklin

- *From Head to Toe*, by Eric Carle

- *I Can, Can You?* by Marjorie Pitzer

- *One, Two, Three . . . Climb!* by Carol Thompson

- *We're Going on a Bear Hunt*, by Michael Rosen, illustrated by Helen Oxenbury

Enhance My Fine Motor Skills

- *Busy Fingers*, by C.W. Bowie, illustrated by Fred Willingham

- *Hands Can*, by Cheryl Willis Hudson, photographs by John-Francis Bourke

- *Hand, Hand, Fingers, Thumb*, by Al Perkins, illustrated by Eric Gurney

- *My First Signs: American Sign Language*, illustrated by Annie Kubler

- *Press Here*, by Hervé Tullet

- *See, Touch, Feel: A First Sensory Book*, by Roger Priddy

- *Ten Little Fingers and Ten Little Toes*, by Mem Fox, illustrated by Helen Oxenbury

- *The Very Hungry Caterpillar*, by Eric Carle

- *Whose Toes Are Those?* by Jabari Asim, illustrated by LeUyen Pham

Teach Me About My Body in Space

- *Belly Button Book!* by Sandra Boynton

- *C Is for Consent*, by Eleanor Morrison, illustrated by Faye Orlove

- *Eyes, Nose, Fingers, and Toes*, by Judy Hindley, illustrated by Brita Granström

- *Look and Learn: All About Me*, by National Geographic Kids

- *The Mitten*, by Jan Brett

- *Poke-a-Dot: What's Your Favorite Color?* by Melissa & Doug

- *Shake My Sillies Out*, by Raffi, illustrated by Maple Lam

- *Whose Knees Are These?* by Jabari Asim, illustrated by LeUyen Pham

References

AAP (American Academy of Pediatrics). 2010. "Prevention of Choking Among Children." *Pediatrics* 125 (3): 601–7. https://pediatrics.aappublications.org/content/125/3/601.full.

Adolph, K.E., & S.R. Robinson. 2015. "Motor Development." Chap. 4 in *Cognitive Processes*, eds. L.S. Liben & U. Müller, 113–57. Vol. 2 of *Handbook of Child Psychology and Developmental Science,* 7th ed., ed. R.M. Lerner. Hoboken, NJ: John Wiley & Sons.

Archer, C., & I. Siraj. 2015. *Encouraging Physical Development Through Movement-Play.* London: Sage Publications.

Bambach, S., L.B. Smith, D.J. Crandall, & C. Yu. 2016. "Objects in the Center: How the Infant's Body Constrains Infant Scenes." Paper presented at the 6th Annual Joint IEEE International Conference on Development and Learning and Epigenetic Robotics, in Cergy-Pontoise, France.

Baker, L., & A. Futterman. 2013. "Grow a Salad! Preschoolers Plant and Prepare Their Food." *Teaching Young Children* 6 (4): 18–21.

Bandura, A. 1976. *Social Learning Theory.* Upper Saddle River, NJ: Prentice-Hall.

Batcha, B. 2005. "Age-by-Age Growth: Milestone Madness." *Parents*, October 5. www.parents.com/baby/development/growth/age-by-age-growth-milestone-madness.

Bergen, D., R. Reid, & L. Torelli. 2008. *Educating and Caring for Very Young Children: The Infant/Toddler Curriculum.* 2nd ed. New York: Teachers College Press.

Berk, L.E., & A.B. Meyers. 2015. *Infants, Children, and Adolescents.* 8th ed. Upper Saddle River, NJ: Pearson.

Better Kid Care. 2016. "Developing Memory." Tip sheet. State College, PA: Better Kids Care, PennState Extension, The Pennsylvania State University. http://bkc-od-media.vmhost.psu.edu/documents/tips1309.pdf.

Better Kid Care. 2019. "Loose Parts: What Does This Mean?" Tip sheet. State College, PA: Better Kids Care, PennState Extension, The Pennsylvania State University. https://extension.psu.edu/programs/betterkidcare/early-care/tip-pages/all/loose-parts-what-does-this-mean.

Bjorklund, D.F., & K.B. Causey. 2017. *Children's Thinking: Cognitive Development and Individual Differences.* 6th ed. Thousand Oaks, CA: Sage Publications.

Bodrova, E., & D.J. Leong. 2006. *Tools of the Mind: The Vygotskian Approach to Early Childhood Education.* 2nd ed. Upper Saddle River, NJ: Pearson.

Bongiorno, L. n.d. "Supporting the Development of Creativity." *NAEYC for Families.* www.naeyc.org/our-work/families/supporting-development-creativity.

Brazelton, T.B., & J.D. Sparrow. 2006. *Touchpoints—Birth to Three.* 2nd ed. Boston: Da Capo Press.

Bronson, M.B. 1995. *The Right Stuff for Children Birth to 8: Selecting Play Materials to Support Development.* Washington, DC: NAEYC.

Brooker, L. 2016. "Making This My Space: Infants' and Toddlers' Use of Resources to Make a Day Care Setting Their Own." In *Lived Spaces of Infant-Toddler Education and Care: Exploring Diverse Perspectives on Theory, Research, and Practice,* eds. L.J. Harrison & J. Sumsion, 29–42. New York: Springer.

Brownell, C.A., J. Drummond, S. Hammond, S. Nichols, G. Ramani, E. Satlof-Bedrick, M. Svetlova, W. Waugh, & S. Zerwas. 2016. "Prosocial Behavior in Infancy: The Role of Socialization." *Child Development Perspectives* 10 (4): 222–7.

Brownell, C.A., & C.B. Kopp, eds. 2007. *Socioemotional Development in the Toddler Years: Transitions and Transformations*. New York: Guilford Press.

Brownell, C.A., S. Zerwas, & G.B. Ramani. 2007. "'So Big': The Development of Body Self-Awareness in Toddlers." *Child Development* 78 (5): 1426–40.

Bryant, S. 2014. "Music and Toddlers: Benefits of Music and Movement in Early Childhood." *NAMM Foundation*, June 1. www.nammfoundation.org/articles/2014-06-01/music -and-toddlers-benefits-music-and-movement-early-childhood.

Case-Smith, J. 2010. "Development of Childhood Occupations." In *Occupational Therapy for Children*, 6th ed., eds. J. Case-Smith & J.C. O'Brien, 56–83. Maryland Heights, MO: Mosby Elsevier.

CDC (Centers for Disease Control and Prevention). 2020. "Animals in Schools and Daycare Settings." *Centers for Disease Control and Prevention: Healthy Pets, Healthy People*, last modified August 11. www.cdc.gov/features/animalsinschools/index.html.

CDE (California Department of Education). 2009. *California Infant/Toddler Learning and Development Foundations*. Sacramento: CDE. www.cde.ca.gov/sp/cd/re/documents /itfoundations2009.pdf.

Center on the Developing Child. n.d. "What Is Early Childhood Development? A Guide to the Science." *Center on the Developing Child, Harvard University.* https://developingchild .harvard.edu/resources/five-numbers-to-remember-about-early-childhood-development.

Coleman, P.A. 2020. "The Importance of Playing with a Child's Sense of Smell." *Fatherly*, last modified September 22. www.fatherly.com/parenting/importance-playing-childs -sense-smell.

Cooper, P. 2009. *The Classrooms All Young Children Need: Lessons in Teaching from Vivian Paley*. Chicago: University of Chicago Press.

Daly, L., & M. Beloglovsky. 2016. *Loose Parts 2: Inspiring Play with Infants and Toddlers*. St. Paul, MN: Redleaf Press.

Davis, P.E., E. Meins, & C. Fernyhough. 2013. "Individual Differences in Children's Private Speech: The Role of Imaginary Companions." *Journal of Experimental Child Psychology* 116 (3): 561–71.

Dean, A., & L. Gillespie. 2015. "Why Teaching Infants and Toddlers Is Important." *Young Children* 70 (5): 94–6.

Degotardi, S. 2017. "Joint Attention in Infant-Toddler Early Childhood Programs: Its Dynamics and Potential for Collaborative Learning." *Contemporary Issues in Early Childhood* 18 (4): 409–21.

Dewey, J. [1922] 2018. *Democracy and Education: An Introduction to the Philosophy of Education*. Hollywood, FL: Simon & Brown.

Dewey, J. [1938] 1997. *Experience and Education*. New York: Free Press.

DiCarlo, C.F., S.B. Stricklin, & D.H. Reid. 2006. "Increasing Toy Play Among Toddlers with and Without Disabilities by Modifying the Structural Quality of the Classroom Environment." *NHSA Dialog: A Research-to-Practice Journal for the Early Intervention Field* 9 (1): 49–62.

Driver, J. 2011. "Baby Body Language: Want to Know What Baby Is Saying?" *Psychology Today*, June 3. www.psychologytoday.com/us/blog/you-say-more-you-think/201106 /baby-body-language.

Dvorsky, G. 2013. "The Human Nose Can Sense 10 Basic Smells." *Gizmodo*, September 20. https://io9.gizmodo.com/the-human-nose-can-sense-10-basic-smells-1355489504.

Early Childhood Art Educators Issues Group. n.d. "Art: Essential for Early Learning." Position paper. Alexandria, VA: National Art Education Association. https:// arteducators-prod.s3.amazonaws.com/documents/428/70c44f06-64c6-47d0-ae5a -82896c6c0066.pdf?1452797140.

ECLKC (Head Start Early Childhood Learning and Knowledge Center). 2020. "Individualizing Care for Infants and Toddlers." Last modified December 7. https:// eclkc.ohs.acf.hhs.gov/teaching-practices/individualizing-care-infants-toddlers /individualizing-care-infants-toddlers.

Eisner, E.W. 2002. "What Can Education Learn from the Arts About the Practice of Education?" *Journal of Curriculum and Supervision* 18 (1): 4–16.

Engineering Emily. 2018. "Exploring the Five Senses for Babies, Toddlers, and Preschoolers: Sense of Taste." *Engineering Emily* (blog), October 23. www.engineeringemily.com /exploring-the-five-senses-for-babies-toddlers-and-preschoolers-sense-of-taste.

Erikson, E. [1950] 2013. *Childhood and Society*. 2nd ed. New York: W.W. Norton.

Farzin, F., C. Hou, & A.M. Norcia. 2012. "Piecing It Together: Infants' Neural Responses to Face and Object Structure." *Journal of Vision* 12 (13): 6.

Feeney, S., & E. Moravcik. 1987. "A Thing of Beauty: Aesthetic Development in Young Children." *Young Children* 42 (6): 7–15.

Feierabend, J.M. 2019. "Music and Movement for Infants and Toddlers: Naturally Wonder-full." *Feierabend Association for Music Education*. www.feierabendmusic.org /first-steps-in-music-for-infants-and-toddlers.

Feliu-Torruella, M., M. Fernández-Santín, & J. Atenas. 2021. "Building Relationships Between Museums and Schools: Reggio Emilia as a Bridge to Educate Children About Heritage." *Sustainability* 13 (7): 3713.

Forman, G., & E. Hall. 2005. "Wondering with Children: The Importance of Observation in Early Education." *Early Childhood Research and Practice* 7 (2): e1–e11.

Fox, J.E., & R. Schirrmacher. 2014. *Art and Creative Development for Young Children*. 8th ed. Boston: Cengage Learning.

Geher, G., K. Betancourt, & O. Jewell. 2017. "The Link Between Emotional Intelligence and Creativity." *Imagination, Cognition, and Personality* 37 (1): 5–22.

Geist, K., E.A. Geist, & K. Kuznik. 2012. "The Patterns of Music: Young Children Learning Mathematics Through Beat, Rhythm, and Melody." *Young Children* 67 (1): 74–9.

Gerber, M. n.d. "Magda Quotes." *Magda Gerber, Seeing Babies with New Eyes*. www.magdagerber.org/magda-quotes.html.

Gerber, M. 2003. *Dear Parent: Caring for Infants with Respect*. 2nd ed. Los Angeles: Resources for Infant Educarers.

Gerber, R.J., T. Wilks, & C. Erdie-Lalena. 2010. "Developmental Milestones: Motor Development." *Pediatrics in Review* 31 (7): 267–77.

Gill, S.V., K.E. Adolph, & B. Vereijken. 2009. "Change in Action: How Infants Learn to Walk Down Slopes." *Developmental Science* 12 (6): 888–902.

Gillespie, L.G. 2015. "Rocking and Rolling—It Takes Two: The Role of Co-Regulation in Building Self-Regulation Skills." *Young Children* 70 (3): 94–6.

Gillespie, L.G., & J.D. Greenberg. 2017. "Rocking and Rolling: Empowering Infants' and Toddlers' Learning Through Scaffolding." *Young Children* 72 (2): 90–3.

Goouch, K., & S. Powell. 2013. *The Baby Room: Principles, Policy, and Practice*. London: Open University Press.

Gopnik, A. 2009. *The Philosophical Baby: What Children's Minds Tell Us About Truth, Love, and the Meaning of Life*. London: Bodley Head.

Gopnik, A. 2013. "What Do Babies Think?" Interview by Guy Raz. *TED Radio Hour*. KAWC. www.kawc.org/post/what-do-babies-think.

Hadders-Algra, M. 2010. "Variation and Variability: Keywords in Human Motor Development." *Physical Therapy* 90 (12): 1823–37.

Hadders-Algra, M. 2018. "Early Human Motor Development: From Variation to the Ability to Vary and Adapt." *Neuroscience and Biobehavioral Reviews* 90 (July): 411–27.

Haywood, K.M., & N. Getchell. 2014. *Lifespan Motor Development*. 6th ed. Champaign, IL: Human Kinetics.

Helm, J., & L. Katz. 2016. *Young Investigators: The Project Approach in the Early Years*. 3rd ed. New York: Teachers College Press.

Hewett, I. 2013. "Why Lullabies Really Do Send Babies to Sleep." *The Telegraph*, October 30. www.telegraph.co.uk/culture/music/classicalmusic/10412984/Why-lullabies-really -do-send-babies-to-sleep.html.

HHS (US Department of Health and Human Services). 2018. "Infant/Toddler Resource Guide." *Early Childhood Training and Technical Assistance System*. https://childcareta .acf.hhs.gov/infant-toddler-resource-guide/planning-individual-infants-and-toddlers -group-care.

Hirsch, E.S. 1996. *The Block Book*. 3rd ed. Washington, DC: NAEYC.

Huffman, J.M., & C. Fortenberry. 2011. "Developing Fine Motor Skills." *Young Children* 66 (5): 100–3.

Hyson, M. 2008. *Enthusiastic and Engaged Learners: Approaches to Learning in the Early Childhood Classroom*. New York: Teachers College Press.

Hyson, M., & A. Douglas. 2019. "More than Academics: Supporting the Whole Child." In *The Wiley Handbook of Early Childhood Care and Education*, eds. C.P. Brown, M.B. McMullen, & N. File, 279–99. Hoboken, NJ: John Wiley & Sons.

Jones, E.J.H., & J.S. Herbert. 2006. "Exploring Memory in Infancy: Deferred Imitation and the Development of Declarative Memory." *Infant and Child Development* 15 (2): 195–205.

Jung, J., & S. Recchia. 2013. "Scaffolding Infants' Play Through Empowering and Individualizing Teaching Practices." *Early Education and Development* 24 (6): 829–50.

Jung, M., P. Kloosterman, & M.B. McMullen. 2007. "Young Children's Natural Intuition for Solving Problems in Mathematics: A Research in Review." *Young Children* 62 (5): 50–7.

Kanemaru, N., H. Watanabe, & G. Taga. 2012. "Increasing Selectivity of Interlimb Coordination During Spontaneous Movements in 2- to 4-Month-Old Infants." *Experimental Brain Research* 218 (1): 49–61.

Karasik, L.B., K.E. Adolph, C.S. Tamis-LeMonda, & A.L. Zuckerman. 2012. "Carry On: Spontaneous Object Carrying in 13-Month-Old Crawling and Walking Infants." *Developmental Psychology* 48 (2): 389–97.

Karl, J.M., L.-A.R. Sacrey, & I.Q. Whishaw. 2018. "Multiple Motor Channel Theory and the Development of Skilled Hand Movements in Human Infants." In *Reach-to-Grasp Behavior: Brain, Behavior, and Modelling Across the Life Span*, eds. D. Corbetta & M. Santello, 42–68. Abingdon, UK: Routledge Taylor & Francis.

Kile, N.C. 2018. "Baby Picasso: Art with Infants and Toddlers." Online course. Houston: Continued Early Childhood Education. www.continued.com/early-childhood-education /articles/baby-picasso-art-with-infants-22866.

Kimmerle, M., C.L. Ferre, K.A. Kotwica, & G.F. Michel. 2010. "Development of Role-Differentiated Bimanual Manipulation During the Infant's First Year." *Developmental Psychobiology* 52 (2): 168–80.

Kogan, Y., & J. Pin. 2009. "Beginning the Journey: The Project Approach with Toddlers." *Early Childhood Research and Practice* 11 (1): e1–e6.

Kohn, A. 2004. *What Does It Mean to Be Well Educated? And More Essays on Standards, Grading, and Other Follies*. Boston: Beacon Press.

Kolodziej, L. 2015. *Model-Directed Learning: Albert Bandura's Social Cognitive Learning Theory and Its Social-Psychological Significance for School and Instruction*. Munich: GRIN Verlag.

Kuhl, P. 2011. "The Linguistic Genius of Babies." Talk presented and filmed at a TEDxRainier event in Seattle, WA. www.youtube.com/watch?v=G2XBIkHW954.

Lake, A. 2017. "The First 1,000 Days: A Singular Window of Opportunity." *UNICEF Connect* (blog), January 18. https://blogs.unicef.org/blog/first-1000-days-singular-opportunity.

Lally, J.R. 2008. *Caring for Infants and Toddlers in Groups: Developmentally Appropriate Practice*. 2nd ed. Washington, DC: ZERO TO THREE.

Lally, J.R., & P.L. Mangione. 2006. "The Uniqueness of Infancy Demands a Responsive Approach to Care." *Young Children* 61 (4): 14–20.

Lansbury, J. 2009. "Set Me Free—Unrestricted Babies (and the Equipment They Don't Need)." *Janet Lansbury: Elevating Child Care*, September 12. www.janetlansbury.com/2009/09/set-me-free.

LeeKeenan, D., & C.P. Edwards. 1992. "Using the Project Approach with Toddlers." *Young Children* 47 (4): 31–5.

Lerner, C., & R. Parlakian. 2016. "Beyond Twinkle, Twinkle: Using Music with Infants and Toddlers." *ZERO TO THREE*, August 11. www.zerotothree.org/resources/1514-beyond-twinkle-twinkle-using-music-with-infants-and-toddlers.

Lexico, s.v. "Drama." n.d. Accessed February 1, 2021. www.lexico.com/en/definition/drama.

Lieberman, A.F. 2017. *The Emotional Life of the Toddler*. New York: Simon & Schuster.

LoBue, V. 2016. "Face Time: Here's How Infants Learn from Facial Expressions." *The Conversation*, January 26. www.theconversation.com/face-time-heres-how-infants-learn-from-facial-expressions-53327.

Louv, R. 2008. *Last Child in the Woods: Saving Our Children from Nature-Deficit Disorder*. Chapel Hill, NC: Algonquin Books.

Loveless, B. n.d. "Observational Learning: The Complete Guide." *Education Corner*. www.educationcorner.com/observational-learning-guide.html.

Mangione, P.L., J.R. Lally, & S. Signer. 1990. *The Ages of Infancy: Caring for Young, Mobile, and Older Infants*. Sacramento: CDE Press.

Marinovich, A., host. 2016. "Using Puppets with Infants and Toddlers." *Learn with Less* (podcast), May 6. www.learnwithless.com/podcast/become-a-puppeteer.

McClelland, M.M., & S.L. Tominey. 2014. "The Development of Self-Regulation and Executive Function in Young Children." *ZERO TO THREE* 35 (2): 1–8.

McMullen, M.B. 1998. "Thinking Before Doing: A Giant Toddler Step on the Road to Literacy." *Young Children* 53 (3): 65–70.

McMullen, M.B. 2013. "Understanding Development of Infants and Toddlers." In *Developmentally Appropriate Practice: Focus on Infants and Toddlers*, eds. C. Copple, S. Bredekamp, D. Koraleck, & K. Charner, 23–50. Washington, DC: NAEYC.

McMullen, M.B. 2018. "The Multiple Benefits of Continuity of Care for Infants and Toddlers, Families, and Caregiving Staff." *Young Children* 73 (3): 38–42.

McMullen, M.B., J. Addleman, A.M. Fulford, S. Mooney, S. Moore, S. Sisk, & J. Zachariah. 2009. "Learning to Be *Me* While Coming to Understand *We*: Encouraging Prosocial Babies in Group Settings." *Young Children* 64 (4): 20–8.

McMullen, M.B., C. Buzzelli, & N.R. Yun. 2016. "Pedagogy of Care for Well-Being." In *The Routledge International Handbook of Philosophies and Theories of Early Childhood Education and Care*, eds. T. David, K. Goouch, & S. Powell, 259–68. London: Taylor and Francis.

Menzer, M. 2015. *The Arts in Early Childhood: Social and Emotional Benefits of Arts Participation—A Literature Review and Gap-Analysis (2000–2015)*. Report. Washington, DC: National Endowment for the Arts. www.arts.gov/sites/default/files/arts-in-early-childhood-dec2015-rev.pdf.

Munakata, Y., L. Michaelson, J. Barker, & N. Chevalier. 2013. "Executive Functioning During Infancy and Childhood." In *Encyclopedia on Early Childhood Development: Executive Functions*, e1–e5. Quebec City, QC, Canada: Centre of Excellence for Early Childhood Development & Strategic Knowledge Cluster on Early Child Development. www.child-encyclopedia.com/sites/default/files/textes-experts/en/646/executive-functioning-during-infancy-and-childhood.pdf.

Murkoff, H. 2019. "Imaginary Friends and Toddlers." *What to Expect*, February 6. www.whattoexpect.com/toddler/ask-heidi/imaginary-friends.aspx.

NAEYC. 2019a. "Advancing Equity in Early Childhood Education." Position statement. Washington, DC: NAEYC. www.naeyc.org/resources/position-statements/equity.

NAEYC 2019b. "Professional Standards and Competencies for Early Childhood Educators." Position statement. Washington, DC: NAEYC. www.naeyc.org/resources/position -statements/professional-standards-competencies.

NAEYC. 2020. "Developmentally Appropriate Practice." Position statement. Washington, DC: NAEYC. www.naeyc.org/resources/position-statements/dap/contents.

NRC (National Research Council) & IOM (Institute of Medicine). 2000. *From Neurons to Neighborhoods: The Science of Early Childhood Development*. Report. Washington, DC: National Academies Press.

Parks, L. 2015. "Mirrors: Playing with Reflections." *Texas Child Care Quarterly* 39 (2): e1–e4. www.childcarequarterly.com/pdf/fall15_mirrors.pdf.

Partanen, E., T. Kujala, M. Tervaniemi, & M. Huotilainen. 2013. "Prenatal Music Exposure Induces Long-Term Neural Effects." *PLOS One* 8 (10): e78946. doi:10.1371/journal .pone.0078946.

Payne, V.G., & L.D. Isaacs. 2017. *Human Motor Development: A Lifespan Approach*. 9th ed. Abingdon, UK: Routledge.

Piaget, J., & B. Inhelder. 1969. *The Psychology of the Child*. New York: Basic Books.

Price, C.L., & E.A. Steed. 2016. "Culturally Responsive Strategies." *Young Children* 71 (5): 57–66.

Purewal, R., R. Christley, K. Kordas, C. Joinson, K. Meints, N. Gee, & C. Westgarth. 2017. "Companion Animals and Child/Adolescent Development: A Systematic Review of the Evidence." *International Journal of Environmental Research and Public Health* 14 (3): 234–59.

Raising Children Network. 2019. "Talking with Babies and Toddlers: How to Do It and Why." Last modified November 19. www.raisingchildren.net.au/babies/connecting -communicating/communicating/talking-with-babies-toddlers.

Raising Children Network. 2020. "Overstimulation: Babies and Children." Last modified October 30. www.raisingchildren.net.au/newborns/behaviour/common-concerns /overstimulation.

Remitz, J. 2013. "5 Best Classroom Pets." *PetMD*, August 22. www.petmd.com/exotic /slideshows/care/best-classroom-pets.

Rivkin, M.S. 2014. *The Great Outdoors: Advocating for Natural Spaces for Young Children*. Rev. ed. Washington, DC: NAEYC.

Robinson, S.R., & G.A. Kleven. 2005. "Learning to Move Before Birth." In *Prenatal Development of Postnatal Functions*, eds. B. Hopkins & S.P. Johnson, 131–75. Westport, CT: Praeger.

Robinson-O'Brien, R., M. Story, & S. Heim, S. 2009. "Impact of Garden-Based Youth Nutrition Intervention Programs: A Review." *Journal of the American Dietetic Association* 109 (2): 273–80.

Ruff, H., & M. Capozzoli. 2003. "Development of Attention and Distractibility in the First 4 Years of Life." *Developmental Psychology* 39 (5): 877–90.

Rymanowicz, K. 2015. "The Little Toddler That Could: Autonomy in Toddlerhood." *Michigan State University Extension*, February 17. www.canr.msu.edu/news/the _little_toddler_that_could_autonomy_in_toddlerhood.

Schaefer, R. 2016. "Teacher Inquiry on the Influence of Materials on Children's Learning." *Young Children* 71 (5): 64.

Schmidt, R.A., & T.D. Lee. 2011. *Motor Control and Learning: A Behavioral Emphasis*. 5th ed. Champaign, IL: Human Kinetics.

Schwarzenberg, S.J., & M.K. Georgieff. 2018. "Your Baby's First 1,000 Days: AAP Policy Explained." *HealthyChildren.org*, last modified January 22. www.healthychildren.org /English/ages-stages/baby/Pages/Babys-First-1000-Days-AAP-Policy-Explained.aspx.

Semmar, Y., & T. Al-Thani. 2015. "Piagetian and Vygotskian Approaches to Cognitive Development in the Kindergarten Classroom." *Journal of Educational and Developmental Psychology* 5 (2): e1–e7. doi:10.5539/jedp.v5n2p1.

Shin, M. 2012. "The Role of Joint Attention in Social Communication and Play Among Infants." *Journal of Early Childhood Research* 10 (3): 309–17.

Shore, R. 2003. *Rethinking the Brain: New Insights into Early Development.* Rev. ed. New York: Families and Work Institute.

Sobel, D.M., & N.Z. Kirkham. 2006. "Blickets and Babies: The Development of Causal Reasoning in Toddlers and Infants." *Developmental Psychology* 42 (6): 1103–15.

Starr, A., M.E. Libertus, & E.M. Brannon. 2013. "Number Sense in Infancy Predicts Mathematical Abilities in Childhood." *Proceedings of the National Academy of Sciences of the United States of America* 110 (45): 181116–20.

Stiefel, C. 2005. "What Your Child Learns by Imitating You." *Parents*, October 5. www .parents.com/toddlers-preschoolers/development/behavioral/what-your-child-learns -by-imitating-you.

Suddendorf, T., & C.M. Fletcher-Flinn. 2011. "Theory of Mind and the Origin of Divergent Thinking." *Journal of Creative Behavior* 31 (3): 169–79.

Thompson, J.E., & R.A. Thompson. 2007. "Natural Connections: Children, Nature, and Social-Emotional Development." *Exchange* 178: 46–9.

Tominey, S.L., E.C. O'Bryon, S.E. Rivers, & S. Shapeses. 2017. "Teaching Emotional Intelligence in Early Childhood." *Young Children* 72 (1): 6–12.

Tryphon, A., & J. Vonèche, eds. 2016. *Working with Piaget: Essays in Honour of Bärbel Inhelder.* New York: Psychology Press.

United Nations. 1989. "Convention on the Rights of the Child." *Treaty Series* (1577): 3. www.ohchr.org/EN/ProfessionalInterest/Pages/CRC.aspx.

Uprichard, E. 2008. "Children as 'Being' and 'Becomings.'" *Children and Society* 22 (4): 303–13.

Vanover, S.T. 2018. "The Importance of Sand and Water Play." *NAEYC* (blog), July 18. www.naeyc.org/resources/blog/importance-sand-and-water-play.

Vecchi, V. 2010. *Art and Creativity in Reggio Emilia: Exploring the Role and Potential of Ateliers in Early Childhood Education.* Abingdon, UK: Taylor and Francis.

von Hofsten, C., & K. Rosander. 2018. "The Development of Sensorimotor Intelligence in Infants." *Advances in Child Development and Behavior* 55: 73–106.

Vygotsky, L.S. [1930–35] 1978. *The Mind in Society: The Development of Higher Psychological processes.* Ed. and trans. M. Cole, V. John-Steiner, S. Scribner, & E. Souberman. Cambridge, MA: Harvard University Press.

Vygotsky, L.S. 1987. "Thinking and Speech." In *Problems of General Psychology,* eds. R.W. Reiber & A.S. Carton, 37–285. Vol. 1 of *The Collected Works of L.S. Vygotsky.* New York: Plenum.

Vygotsky, L.S. 2004. "Imagination and Creativity in Childhood." *Journal of Russian and East European Psychology* 42 (1): 7–97.

Wanerman, T. 2013. *From Handprints to Hypotheses: Using the Project Approach with Toddlers and Twos.* St. Paul, MN: Redleaf Press.

Warneken, F., & M. Tomasello. 2008. "Extrinsic Rewards Undermine Altruistic Tendencies in 20-Month-Olds." *Developmental Psychology* 44 (6): 1785–8.

Wolff, K., & A. Stapp. 2019. "Investigating Early Childhood Teachers' Perceptions of a Preschool Yoga Program." *SAGE Open* 9 (1): e1–e9. doi:10.1177/2158244018821758.

Xu, F. 2013. "The Object Concept in Human Infants." *Human Development* 56 (3): 167–70.

ZERO TO THREE. 2010a. "24–36 Months: Social-Emotional Development." *ZERO TO THREE,* February 22. www.zerotothree.org/resources/241-24-36-months-social -emotional-development.

ZERO TO THREE. 2010b. "Supporting Thinking Skills from 0–12 Months." *ZERO TO THREE*, May 19. www.zerotothree.org/resources/1282-supporting-thinking-skills-from-0-12-months.

ZERO TO THREE. 2016. "How to Support your Child's Communication Skills." *ZERO TO THREE*, February 25. www.zerotothree.org/resources/302-how-to-support-your-child-s-communication-skills

Zorn, A. 2012. "Toddlerhood: The Load and Tote Phase." *Bounceback Parenting*, June 19. https://bouncebackparenting.com/toddlerhood-the-load-and-tote-phase.

Resources

Books

Birckmayer, J., A. Kennedy, & A. Stonehouse. 2008. *From Lullabies to Literature: Stories in the Lives of Infants and Toddlers.* Washington, DC: NAEYC; Jamberoo, Australia: Pademelon Press.

Brazelton, T.B., & J.D. Sparrow. 2006. *Touchpoints—Birth to Three.* 2nd ed. Boston: Da Capo Press.

Carlson, F.M. 2011. *Big Body Play: Why Boisterous, Vigorous, and Very Physical Play Is Essential to Children's Development and Learning.* Washington, DC: NAEYC.

CDE (California Department of Education). 2009. *California Infant/Toddler Learning and Development Foundations.* Sacramento: CDE.

Cobb, J. 2012. *What'll I Do with the Baby-o? More than 350 Rhymes and Songs to Use in Play with Babies and Toddlers.* Vancouver, BC, Canada: Black Sheep Press.

Daly, L., & M. Beloglovsky. 2016. *Loose Parts 2: Inspiring Play with Infants and Toddlers.* St. Paul, MN: Redleaf Press.

Derman-Sparks, L, & J.O. Edwards. With C.M. Goins. 2020. *Anti-Bias Education for Young Children and Ourselves.* 2nd ed. Washington, DC: NAEYC.

Dombro, A.L., J. Jablon, & C. Stetson. 2020. *Powerful Interactions: How to Connect with Children to Extend Their Learning.* 2nd ed. Washington, DC: NAEYC.

Gandini, L., L. Hill, L.B. Cadwell, & C.S. Schwall, eds. 2015. *In the Spirit of the Studio: Learning from the* Atelier *of Reggio Emilia.* 2nd ed. New York: Teachers College Press.

Gerber, M. 2003. *Dear Parent: Caring for Infants with Respect.* 2nd ed. Los Angeles: Resources for Infant Educarers.

Gerber, M., & A. Johnson. 2012. *Your Self-Confident Baby: How to Encourage Your Child's Natural Abilities—From the Very Start.* Hoboken, NJ: Wiley.

Gonzalez-Mena, J. 2007. *Diversity in Early Care and Education: Honoring Differences.* 5th ed. New York: McGraw-Hill Education.

Gopnik, A. 2009. *The Philosophical Baby: What Children's Minds Tell Us About Truth, Love, and the Meaning of Life.* London: Bodley Head.

Gopnik, A. 2017. *The Gardener and the Carpenter: What the New Science of Child Development Tells Us About the Relationship Between Parents and Children.* London: Picador.

Gopnik, A., A.N. Meltzoff, & P.K. Kuhl. 2000. *The Scientist in the Crib: Minds, Brains, and How Children Learn.* New York: William Morrow.

Greenman, J., A. Stonehouse, & G. Schweikert. 2008. *Prime Times: A Handbook for Excellence in Infant and Toddler Programs.* 2nd ed. St. Paul, MN: Redleaf Press.

Hirsch, E.S. 1996. *The Block Book.* 3rd ed. Washington, DC: NAEYC.

Koralek, D., & L.G. Gillespie, eds. 2011. *Spotlight on Infants and Toddlers.* Washington, DC: NAEYC.

Lally, J.R. 2008. *Caring for Infants and Toddlers in Groups: Developmentally Appropriate Practice.* 2nd ed. Washington, DC: ZERO TO THREE.

Leach, P. 2010. *Your Baby and Child: From Birth to Age Five.* Rev. ed. New York: Knopf.

Lieberman, A.F. 2017. *The Emotional Life of the Toddler.* New York: Simon & Schuster.

Luckenbill, J., A. Subramaniam, & J. Thompson. 2019. *This Is Play: Environments and Interactions that Engage Infants and Toddlers.* Washington, DC: NAEYC.

Solomon, D.C. 2013. *Baby Knows Best: Raising a Confident and Resourceful Child, the RIE Way*. New York: Little, Brown and Company.

Wanerman, T. 2013. *From Handprints to Hypotheses: Using the Project Approach with Toddlers and Twos*. St. Paul, MN: Redleaf Press.

Wittmer, D.S., & A.S. Honig. 2020. *Day to Day the Relationship Way: Creating Responsive Programs for Infants and Toddlers*. Washington, DC: NAEYC.

Online

- **The AAP Parenting Website:** www.healthychildren.org
- **The Abolitionist Teaching Network:** www.abolitionistteachingnetwork.org
- **Childhood Education International:** www.ceinternational1892.org
- **Defending the Early Years:** www.dey.org
- **Diverse Book Finder:** www.diversebookfinder.org
- **Early Head Start:** https://eclkc.ohs.acf.hhs.gov
- **Early Head Start National Resource Center's "Supporting Outdoor Play and Exploration for Infants and Toddlers":** https://eclkc.ohs.acf.hhs.gov/sites/default/files/pdf/ehs-ta-paper-14-outdoor-play.pdf
- **Eartheasy's "Gardening with Children":** https://learn.eartheasy.com/guides/gardening-with-children
- **HighScope's Infant-Toddler Curriculum:** https://highscope.org/our-practice/infant-toddler-curriculum
- **Janet Lansbury | Elevating Child Care:** www.janetlansbury.com
- **Learning for Justice:** www.learningforjustice.org
- **Living Montessori Now's "Montessori for Infants":** www.livingmontessorinow.com/montessori-for-infants
- **National Association for the Education of Young Children (NAEYC):** NAEYC.org
- **NAEYC's "Engaging Toddlers in Nature Play":** NAEYC.org/resources/blog/engaging-toddlers-nature-play
- **National Black Child Development Institute (NBCDI):** www.nbcdi.org
- **National Head Start Association's "Creating and Sustaining Inclusive Environments to Support LGBTQ+ Families":** www.nhsa.org/supporting-lgbtq-families
- **Program for Infant/Toddler Care (PITC):** www.pitc.org
- **Resources for Infant Educarers (RIE):** www.rie.org
- **Scholastic Early Childhood Today's "Infants & Toddlers: Let's Go Outside!":** www.scholastic.com/teachers/articles/teaching-content/infants-toddlers-lets-go-outside
- **Start Early:** www.startearly.org
- **Unidos US's "Education":** www.unidosus.org/issues/education
- **United Nations' "Convention on the Rights of the Child":** www.ohchr.org/EN/ProfessionalInterest/Pages/CRC.aspx
- **US Department of Health and Human Services' "Infant/Toddler Resource Guide":** https://childcareta.acf.hhs.gov/infant-toddler-resource-guide/planning-individual-infants-and-toddlers-group-care
- **The Virtual Lab School's "The Outdoor Environment: Designing for Engagement":** www.virtuallabschool.org/infant-toddler/learning-environments/lesson-3
- **ZERO TO THREE:** www.zerotothree.org

Index

Acknowledgments

To every child—I dream of a world where you can laugh, dance, sing, learn, live in peace, and be happy.

—Malala Yousafzai (@Malala) on Twitter, November 20, 2017

We wrote this book in celebration of all who care for and educate our youngest citizens. We value and honor the work that you do, the most important work of all, and we hope you find this book helpful.

We thank our families, friends, and colleagues for their support and advice along this journey, and all the children, past and present, who have enriched our lives and taught us so much.

About the Authors

Mary Benson McMullen, PhD, is professor of early childhood education at Indiana University (IU), where she has been on faculty since 1993. She received a BS from Michigan State University and earned MS and PhD degrees in child development from Florida State University. During and after her graduate education, she worked as a teacher of infants, toddlers, and preschoolers and then as an early childhood program director, before accepting her position at IU. At IU, she teaches courses to preservice and in-service early childhood teaching professionals, as well as to doctoral students who plan to become early childhood teacher education scholars. Mary's primary research interests involve factors that influence quality early care and education for infants and toddlers; the healthy overall growth, development, learning, and well-being of young children (birth through age 5); teaching beliefs and practices across cultures and contexts; and factors that influence and ensure the well-being of professionals who care for young children. She has published dozens of articles for both research and teaching journals, as well as numerous book chapters. She is coeditor of the 2019 book *The Wiley Handbook of Early Childhood Care and Education.* Mary lives in Bloomington, Indiana, where she and her husband of 40 years raised their three sons.

Dylan Brody (they/them), MSEd, is a doctoral student at the University of Georgia. They are currently the graduate research assistant for the Department of Educational Theory and Practice, with a focus on critical studies. Dylan began working as a full-time teacher with infants and toddlers in 2010 and fell deeply in love with the complexity of teaching young children. They worked collaboratively with a coteacher in a setting that utilizes a continuity of care model, providing Dylan the space and support needed to build intimate and meaningful connections with children and their families over the course of a three-year cycle. This time allowed them to create a more deeply reflective teaching practice and mindful rapport with families through daily moments of trust building. Dylan's primary research and teaching interests focus on ethics, equity, critical theory, mindfulness, and advocacy for fellow teachers who experience marginalization. They prioritize care practices and policies that allow all members of the community to feel safer to be themselves and challenge the barriers in place that might prevent success for all. Dylan hopes to work more closely in the future with early childhood teachers in the LGBTQ+ community and to further advocate for trans visibility and representation in the field. Dylan currently lives in Athens, Georgia, with their beloved cat, Bean.

More High-Quality Resources for Infant & Toddler Educators

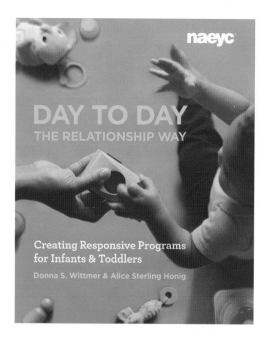

Day to Day the Relationship Way

This book discusses ways teachers can support children's development in all domains through daily relationship-based interactions and highlights the awe-inspiring capabilities of infants and toddlers to learn and love when nurtured through meaningful relationships.

Features include

› A focus on emotional and social development as the foundation for learning
› Research findings that tie to everyday practice
› Engaging vignettes and examples that bring relationship-based program elements to life
› Links with the NAEYC Early Learning Program Accreditation Standards

2020 • 168 pages
Print: ISBN 978-1-938113-55-0 • Item 1142
E-book: ISBN 978-1-938113-56-7 • Item e1142

This Is Play

Slow down, tune in, and discover the very purposeful play of infants and toddlers. Addressing considerations like choosing interesting materials, setting up safe and inviting environments, and why you are the most important element of play for very young children, the authors come alongside to help you

› Better understand what play means for infants and toddlers
› Read children's cues and respond to their needs for more challenge, a break from interaction, or a play partner
› Support children's physical, social and emotional, language, and cognitive development
› Adapt the way you play with children and what materials you offer based on individual abilities, interests, and needs
› Look at toddler behavior in new ways and use proven strategies to help children navigate play situations with peers

2019 • 136 pages
Print: ISBN 978-1-938113-53-6 • Item 1141
E-book: ISBN 978-1-938113-54-3 • Item e1141

Order online at **NAEYC.org/shop** or **1-800-424-2460**